Dr Stefan Buczacki is known to millions as the leading expert on garden pests and diseases. A member of the BBC Radio 4's panel of experts on GARDENER'S QUESTION TIME, he also contributes regularly to the *Guardian, Amateur Gardening,* and *The Gardener* and is the author of many best-selling books on gardening.

GARDEN WARFARE

STEFAN BUCZACKI

SPHERE BOOKS LIMITED

A SPHERE BOOK

First published in Great Britain by Souvenir Press Ltd 1988
Published by Sphere Books Ltd 1989

Printed and bound in Great Britain by
Richard Clay Ltd, Bungay, Suffolk

Sphere Books Ltd
A Division of
Macdonald Group Ltd
1 New Fetter Lane, London EC4P 1AR
A member of Maxwell Pergamon Publishing Corporation plc

Contents

PART ONE
THE INVADING ARMY

1 The Airborne Invaders

Sometimes they arrive by night, sometimes by day. Occasionally you will hear them in flight. Even more occasionally, you will actually see them winging their way towards your garden; and it always is *your* garden to which their inbuilt radar directs them. From the sky, from over the horizon, the airborne invaders come. One moment, your plants are clean, healthy, vigorous; the next, they may be hosts to writhing masses of animate vitality or present a curiously deficient, defective appearance, bereft in an instant of their flowers, buds or parts of their leaves, so they could pass muster as colanders or lace table mats.

I never cease to be astonished at the facility with which representatives of almost all groups of the animal kingdom have taken to living in the third dimension. They have, to use a well-worn phrase, conquered the air in a way that still eludes mere men who can only labour themselves aloft in mechanical contrivances. Although a few creatures have the facility to glide short distances from tree to tree or from tree to ground (the so-called flying squirrels and flying snakes, for instance) using simple flaps of skin, it is the possession of wings that places the truly airborne beasts in a quite separate league. The advantages of wings are fairly self-evident—you can travel further, faster. They enable you to find a mate, to disperse your offspring and, most importantly when someone's garden is the landing ground, to locate new supplies of food. And no one needs to spend very long in a garden before they realise that the vast majority of flying animal life belongs, like the greater number of all garden enemies, to the vast group of insects.

Aside from the generalisation that small animals usually have small wings, there is enormous diversity in the way that wings operate, in the efficiency with which different types of airborne invader actually fly, the distances over which they travel and the frequency with which they go aloft. Some insects, like some birds, spend a large part of their time in the air. Others, like earwigs, fly so infrequently that it comes as a matter of some astonishment when they do take off; a happening that is as unexpected as seeing an Inter-City express suddenly take to the air. And unlike modern, man-made flying devices, most flying insects still rely on double pairs of wings although none have adopted the triple configuration that served the Red Baron so well in his triplane.

On some occasions, airborne troops take off *en masse* and fly together almost in formation, to land in swarms. Fortunately, there are no examples in British gardens to compare remotely with the tropical locusts whose countless millions blacken the sky for hours on end and whose tireless jaws reduce hundreds of square kilometres of vegetation to nought. (Their European relatives, the grasshoppers and crickets, are essentially solitary ground-hopping beasts that pounce around the garden in the manner of underpowered Harriers, munching grass wherever they land like a vertical take-off cow.) Sometimes even long-distance fliers arrive with stealth, in ones and twos, commonly defying international airline regulations and travelling when extremely pregnant or relying on a prodigious sexual appetite that is satiated in the subjugation of the indigenous local population when they arrive. In both of these cases, the end result is the same. The local vegetation is overwhelmed by sheer force of numbers. For if the invaders themselves do not cause much damage, their offspring will. And sometimes, these children of the invaders are flightless individuals whose body processes can thus concentrate to the full on the important business of feeding.

The smallest among the airborne, plant-hunting troops in most gardens are **thrips**, better known as thunder flies from their fondness for swarming in astronomical quantities in warm, humid weather. Their wings are feeble and they do very little actual flying, arriving in your garden and in your hair on thermals and air currents by which they can be transported long distances. Generally, small animals with small wings, like thrips and like **aphids** (also called greenfly or blackfly, although some of them are grey, brown, red or yellow), only do very much actual flying when the wind is slight and they are fairly close to the ground. Rather after the fashion of light-weight, shoulder-launched terrain-hugging missiles, they can make an approach at low level. But given a gust of breeze, they are borne aloft, to be transported glider-style over fences, hedges, railways, motorways, even English Channels; for the wind and the creatures it carries are no respecters of national boundaries. Thrips, aphids and the feeble-flying allies of aphids, the **whiteflies**, are suckers, having their mouthparts modified to form hypodermic styluses with which they suck the sap from their unsuspecting hosts. Once they have landed, the ensuing massed colonies of

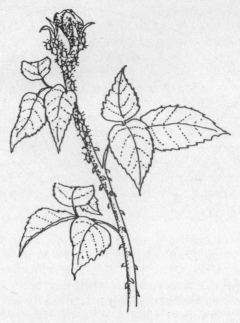

Massed colonies of aphids on a rose shoot.

aphids are usually fairly conspicuous, brazen beasts, although whiteflies are much shyer, preferring to lurk on the undersides of leaves from which they erupt in clouds when disturbed. Thrips tend to form scattered colonies on leaves and flowers, sucking sap from the surface cells only and forming a surface mottling rather than any deep-seated damage.

Larger than the deceptively insidious aphids are whole squadrons of true flies (relatives of the house fly), **sawflies**, **bees**, **wasps**, **ants**, **bugs** and **beetles**. These are often powerfully built strike forces with small but very fast-moving wings that offer great manoeuvrability and in some groups actually enable the owner to indulge in helicopter-like hovering. Most

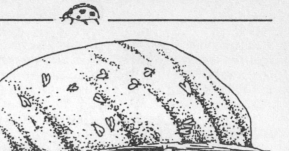

Whiteflies prefer to lurk on the undersides of leaves.

tend to attack and hunt singly, although as in the case of wasps, many individuals can home in to their targets from far and wide, with the result that ripening fruits are festooned with large masses of insects from different bases. Beetles are the most diverse flying machines that have ever graced our planet—there are more species of beetle in the world than of any other insect and the largest forms, like the tropical rhinoceros beetle or even the British cockchafers, really are the heavy bombers of garden warfare. The mere sound of a cockchafer at full speed crashing into a window pane on a warm summer's evening is enough to alert even the most Mainwaring-like of Home Guards. In common with most flying insects, they have two pairs of wings, but the foremost are modified to form protective covers; in some instances, such as the Colorado beetle, attractively marked with squadron-like designations. Having arrived at their destinations, flies, beetles, wasps and their kin set about plant destruction by straightforward mandibular chewing—a technique that ensures a much more rapid demise than the slow, laboured sap-sucking procedure.

Slightly larger wings and a slow, laboured but usually fairly well directed flight pattern characterise **butterflies** and **moths**. Almost all butterflies and many moths are on peaceful civilian flights, but the virginal coloration of the **large white butterfly** is about as innocent as the white anti-radiation paint of a nuclear bomber. For butterflies and moths characterise particularly well those invaders that cause damage not by their own direct action, but because of the voracious offspring that they deposit in the enemy territory. Every female large white butterfly is capable of producing several hundred eggs on arrival, and cabbages will be reduced to shreds in a trice once the caterpillars have emerged.

The largest airborne animals, birds in particular, are much more normally masters or mistresses of their own destiny and are much less dependent on wind-assistance. They arrive in your garden rather than anyone else's because it is your garden they have detected from afar and not because the wind has by chance so directed them. And whilst you will be unfortunate indeed if your garden is host to a whole squadron of **wood pigeons**, smaller birds such as **bullfinches** certainly tend to arrive in groups and work concertedly together. Occasionally, their destructive activities seem utterly wanton and to have no connection with feeding activities or even the conquering of new territory. There are few more frustrating yet seemingly pointless pursuits as that indulged in by **sparrows** that tear apart crocus or primrose flowers and leave the debris littering the ground. And no matter how frequently the invaders are disturbed and sent fluttering back into the sky, assuredly they will return again and join in once more the seemingless endless rain of problems from above.

The destructive activities of bullfinches often seem utterly wanton.

15

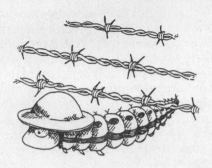

2   The Infiltrators

There is more than one way for an invader to enter a garden. Whilst flying over hedges and the neighbouring countryside might be the most efficient in the short term, the slowly, slowly approach has much to commend it, too. After all, remember the hare and the tortoise. If you invade at ground level and you do it slowly (and you are small), there is much in your favour. No garden can be secured totally, no garden is an island (and even if it were, there would inevitably be water-borne marines to land on the beaches) and no hole is so small that some contingent of the land forces cannot squeeze through it.

The means of locomotion adopted by small, land-based invaders takes several forms. No examples with wheels immediately spring to mind but the origin of the caterpillar track principle will soon stare you in the face. In essence, the means of movement boils down to a distinction between those creatures that do not have legs and those creatures that do, although one significant group offers an intriguing third system in having no legs at all but one large foot. Few legless invaders are likely to be important as damaging influences in most gardens—either because their complete lack of legs renders them too cumbersome to wander far and they take on the role of occupying forces (p. 22) or because they tend to be on our side anyway. Many **nematodes** or **eelworms** are certainly capable of causing havoc once they come into contact with garden plants, and they move by a limited, legless, wriggling, eel-like movement. They comprise a troglodytic army of galactic proportions but their very small size must limit their usefulness as storm troops. The average eelworm is only about one millimetre long, and to travel even the ten metres necessary to attack my potatoes from a base in my neighbour's allotment, would surely require it to possess some form of subterranean rocketry.

Effectively to conduct a campaign over any appreciable distance requires a means of transport above rather than under the soil, and **slugs** and **snails** are the only successful legless exponents of such warfare. They and their fellow molluscs have adopted a unique means of propulsion that comprises a large muscular foot. By regular contractions of this organ, they are able to travel fair distances but once again cannot really operate as a spear-head battalion. Rather they adopt the guerilla role of a border banditry force, lying under the cover of nearby vegetation during the day and striking out through hedges and over fences once darkness has fallen. Then they bring into play one of the most ferociously destructive weapons seen since the Romans abandoned the ballista. The rasping, toothed tongue, called a radula, makes swift work of almost any vegetation in its path and, to add insult to the injury, a glistening slimy trail remains like some obscene graffiti wherever the troops have passed. Snails

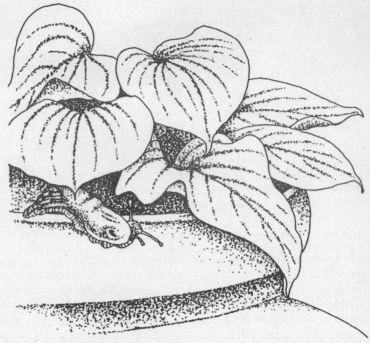

Slugs, the border banditry, wield a weapon of ferocious destructiveness.

differ principally from slugs in their possession of a portable bivouac which serves them in good stead as a temporary shelter when the going becomes too rough. Unfortunately it is of no value against an attacker that is large enough to pick them up wholesale, bivouac and all.

If they have been delivered none too accurately into the next door plot by airborne invaders, **caterpillars** often use their legs to complete the journey into *your* garden. But whilst having the obligatory six legs of other insects, they are faced with something of a mobility problem in the amount of legless bodywork that could sag embarrassingly. The problem is neatly circumvented by an additional undercarriage of up to

18

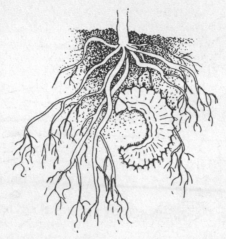

The fat, smug vine weevil larva, menace of soil-less composts.

five pairs of fleshy, jointless prolegs that give extra support aft. The precise means by which these various legs are brought into play can range from a fairly conventional walking posture to an assertive, ground-gobbling, looping action, complete with dramatic warpaint and a gigantic, hairy head-dress. Caterpillars in fact exemplify rather well the two extreme approaches to visibility adopted by armies of all kinds. Whilst some employ the 'terrify your enemy into keeping away' approach and are painted so brightly and aggressively that they would be missed only by the blind, others adopt subtle and ingenious camouflage. Sometimes this is to blend them with surrounding plant life, but sometimes the disguise is a blatant attempt to confuse by appearing similar to some other, innocuous or poisonous creature. Caterpillars are not the only infiltrating larvae. The fat, smug **vine weevil** is another, the gift to gardening of its flightless parents and a creature that has recently made soil-less composts very much its home.

Whilst few types of mature insect are wingless (female

scale insects are notable exceptions), many **beetles**, amongst others, appear to have abandoned air travel as a routine invasion tactic and prefer to use their long and efficient legs to move rapidly across the ground. Nonetheless, they appear to have lost the gregarious habit too and as more or less solitary marauding mercenaries, rarely achieve much importance in the overall battle for the garden.

By adding two more legs to an insect, we create an **arachnid**. Most of these eight-legged individuals are on our side (see p. 81), but the group also includes some extremely efficient, if minute, enemy land forces. They are called **mites** and the majority really are so small and so inconspicuous that they have tended to act most effectively in a guerilla role. Nonetheless, land based invasions of **red spider** and other mites can sometimes occur, although perhaps the commonest way for them to arrive in the garden is through utilising the time honoured Trojan horse principle, secreted within newly bought plants.

It is when we move up in leg numbers that some of the most efficient of all land-based troops are encountered, and what they seem to lack in intelligence, they make up for in sheer force of numbers. **Woodlice** have several legs—up to fourteen, depending on the species—and they also have a rather ingenious jointed armour plating that has certainly stood the test of time. For trilobites, distant relatives of modern woodlice, were using essentially the same system to protect themselves in the Cambrian sea over 500 million years ago, and it is only the advent of modern chemical weaponry that has rendered the armour at all vulnerable. To be uncharitable, the woodlouse is old-fashioned, a vestige of a more cumbersome, lumbering age of warfare. They really are little more sophisticated than mere spray-gun fodder, and I always think of them as among the most brainless of the enemies that we have to face. But they reproduce rapidly, producing no larval stage, but young that are miniatures of their parents. Woodlice tend to be night fighters, staggering from their

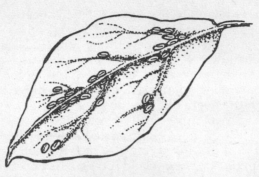

Scale insects in action.

hiding places at dusk to set out on maurading cross-border raids, staggering back again as dawn breaks. They are not sufficiently quick-witted to use anywhere very subtle to hide, nor do they seem to have either fuel capacity or inclination to maraud very far.

At the top of the leg-count league are the **millepedes** which possess, not a thousand legs, but certainly up to one hundred, appreciably more than their relatives the **centipedes** which, of course, are on our side. Millepedes have an undeniably beautiful walking action, a wave motion passing down their sides as, trireme-like, they glide into battle. But you cannot afford to admire the mode of transport for long as their purpose is destructive—any soft, fleshy vegetation such as bulbs or corms that comes their way will be devoured with astonishing efficiency. Whilst the commonest millepedes are fairly readily visible and recognisable as black, superficially snake-like animals, the most destructive are actually smaller, paler and spotted. They tend to operate in a rather similar way to woodlice, ranging over fairly short distances and similarly curling into a more or less armoured ball when attacked, but they never seem quite so innately dim-witted.

21

3 The Occupying Forces

Trying to prevent an invader from landing or crossing the border is one thing; trying to root him out once he is entrenched in your garden is quite another, because occupying forces will consider that the territory has become as much their home as yours. Much is in their favour because, unlike an invading army, they have no problems of long supply lines. Moreover, their families and loved ones may have been brought with them (or, perish the thought, they may even have fraternised and paired up with some of your own kin).

Who or what are these occupiers, and how did they first arrive in your garden? They may perhaps fall into one of the invading categories that I have described already: they could be large, small, free-flying, creeping or crawling. They may have come across the border in unnoticed ones and twos—for who will bother about the odd ant, the single beetle or even the lonesome caterpillar as it wanders through the hedge bottom or over the fence? Of course, no one will, but if the invasion of the odd one or two is repeated several hundred or thousand times over a period of weeks or months, a veritable army can arrive virtually unremarked. Alternatively, the odd two could be a breeding pair or the odd one a sex-starved individual on the look-out for a like-minded partner. And with the fecundity of many invading pests, one plus one can equal many thousand. So the occupiers could be nothing more or less than stealthy, lucky or extremely cunning animal invaders.

Alternatively, they could be animals such as the **nematodes** that I mentioned on p. 17, with such a laborious method of locomotion that it is most improbable they could ever have arrived of their own volition. Thus, they must have been in your garden for a very long time indeed, probably having come initially by the piggy-back or Trojan horse method in soil or on imported plants.

But far and away the largest, most important and most problematic of all occupying forces are those that have some moral grounds for considering the territory of your garden, any garden, their own. They are perfectly content to do battle with their own kith and kin, for these occupiers are not animals at all but other plants. Seen outside the boundaries of your own territory, almost any enemy can appear innocuous, or even attractive and appealing. Wild flowers in the hedgerows and fields are admired by almost everyone, and both national and international laws protect them from harm. But the same attractive plants growing in your own garden tend to take on a different name; one man's terrorists are another's freedom fighters and so the wild flower in a garden becomes a weed.

With very few exceptions of quite unsurpassed nastiness, most occupying weeds do not do battle with garden plants head on. The exceptions, however, include the stranglers—

Bindweed will take on anything in its lustful but deadly embrace.

bindweed, for instance, will gladly take on anything in its lustful but deathly embrace. I think, however, that I may excuse the sweetly perfumed **honeysuckle** that really does seem to kill only through kindness and whose enveloping is harmless enough to plants of its own size, but which sometimes forgets itself and clasps some youngster to its bosom with unfortunate consequences. Less immediately noxious than the stranglers, but much more numerous and almost as effective, are the smotherers. The **ivy** that not only 'hangs by the wall' but on pretty well anything else in its path is typical of smotherers in its patience. Not for them the quick sabre-thrust or the short, sharp shock, but a little by little subjugation of the foe that can last years; the smotherer will wait just as long as it takes. But before leaving the face-to-face brigade, I suppose I must mention too the vampiric **mistletoe** that grows on trees, feasting itself by inserting a root-like organ actually into their tissues, and the somewhat similarly endowed but terrestrial **broomrapes** that dine on the root contents of other plants.

But most occupying weeds are not so objectionable. Theirs is the technique of subduing our plants by patient education; by showing quite clearly that it is they who are better able, better fitted to make use of the resources that our garden environment has to offer. Nonetheless, although they may be educators, their manners are often rough and their approach unsubtle or bullying; like that of many other armies before them. They have essentially the same requirements for food, water and light as does our chosen vegetation. They tend, however, to grow bigger or faster, largely because their ancestors have had countless centuries to become accustomed, adapted to our land. We, for curious reasons of our own, choose to grow primarily plants from other lands, plants that have been thrust into the alien environment of a garden with little warning, and certainly with no time to adapt to a strange diet, or indeed, as I shall mention again, to obtain inoculations against the diseases that may befall them. All in all, a garden plant is ill-prepared to take on any sort of native tribe, and even if a scorched earth policy with spade or powered cultivator enables it to set up home, the indigenous population will very soon reappear to reclaim their birthright.

There are two principal ways in which an occupying weed actually occupies. First, it may be a long-lived creature with some means of protecting itself against any eradication method. Gardeners usually refer to such weeds as perennial, although in many instances, immortal would seem more appropriate. The means to the end of immortality vary—

The apparently immortal couch grass reaches far down into the soil and holds on for dear life.

some weeds like **couch grass** or **ground elder** reach far and deeply into the soil, holding on for dear life when an attempt is made to remove them and having the ingenious facility of shedding parts of their bodies and regenerating new individuals from them. Others, such as the robust and well-armoured **bramble**, yomp across the garden, setting up camp each time they touch ground. And there are also those, like the dreaded pink **oxalis**, that produce tiny packages of vitality called bulbils which spread with the wind and give rise to new plants wherever they land. The alternative to the immortal individual is one with an extremely healthy sex-life—one that can reproduce its kind at an astonishing speed and in a highly indiscriminate fashion. As individuals they last but a season, although it is truly a short life and a very cheerful one. And as is so often found with other species, the real sexual powerhouses among them are often small and insignificant of appearance. Take **chickweed** or the little **hairy bittercress** for example, as petite and charming things as you will find anywhere. But bittercress, to borrow an appropriate description from the Marx Brothers, is a real wolf in lamb's underwear, producing seed at a prodigious rate and flinging it outwards with careless abandon. When such an annual weed produces seed that can germinate almost immediately with no requirement for a dormant period, several generations can occur within a single year and the occupying force then becomes a highly efficient outfit indeed. And truly there are occupying weeds that seem almost the ultimate in fighting machinery—the **groundsel**, for instance, can still reproduce itself and bear seeds after it has been decapitated.

Among wild plants there are some that have adapted to the

Chickweed, small and insignificant but prodigal with its seeds.

role of weed, while others have had it thrust upon them when their own environment was conquered and made a garden. But there are also those such as the **field poppy** that appear to have been born to occupy. Like the brown rat around human dwellings, the poppy has so perfectly adapted to the presence of the disturbed soil that man creates that it hardly ever occurs away from cultivated land and its original wild habitat is obscure. Yes, in one form or another, the occupiers, like the poor, are always with us. You may keep out invaders, but the ability of seeds to remain viable for thirty or more years will always ensure that every garden has at least some undesirable troops in its midst, either rampant at the soil surface or lying dormant beneath it and awaiting their turn to be activated into battle.

4 Tank Regiments

Just as might is not necessarily right, so large size is not always an advantage in warfare of any sort. A large object, animal or army is almost inevitably a conspicuous one. You can see a regiment approaching much sooner than you can see a small squad of infantrymen—if indeed, you see a really small enemy at all before it is too late. A large enemy is very often a noisy one, too, and the sound of your foe crashing through the undergrowth can be an excellent early warning device to alert the national defences. But against all of this must be set several features that are very much in the favour of the invaders. A large, heavy enemy can do a quite enormous amount of purely physical harm simply by walking across your garden. For this is a fragile environment, usually occupied by a high proportion of small, delicate residents quite unable to stand up to lumbering war-horses. Large feet, even if not shod in military boots, can flatten tender vegetation in a trice. Moreover, even a large enemy with gentle pads can have a large appetite and be perfectly capable of devouring as much at one sitting as hundreds of caterpillars would savour for a week.

I call all such massive items of warring flesh the tank regiments, although I accept that they range from the truly gigantic front-line battle tanks, through moderately large, self-propelled guns to highly mobile, lightly weaponed but fleet-footed armoured cars. I am sure that the size range between these larger foes is no greater in proportion than the difference between say, a mite and a caterpillar, but with a nimble field vole at one end of the spectrum and a herd of cows at the other, it certainly seems so. Yes, I think the **cow**, even the solitary cow, is physically the greatest single adversary that any garden ever has to face, but it does come into rather a different category from the conventional fighting machine. For all cows are notionally on our side; I have never encountered an instance where a cow was deliberately turned against or into a garden and perhaps it is best considered not a fighting vehicle at all, but rather in the category of the JCB or road roller pressed unwittingly into military service. The damage caused even by a single errant cow is nonetheless quite monstrous; hoof prints made with the full force of 800kg of flesh can cause total havoc on a lawn, and the plant able to withstand such an impact without incurring serious if not fatal wounds has yet to be invented. In fact, in many instances, the body is unlikely ever to be found and I have known cases where, following impact with a passing hoof, small saxifrages and species irises could only be listed as 'missing in action'.

Given that the cow is really an item of industrial equipment being misused, the **deer** by contrast is a very subtle form of armoured vehicle. Exceptionally well armed with strong teeth and a fairly insatiable appetite, it has the additional attribute of quite phenomenal mobility, being able to clear a height of at least one and a half metres. But at least deer are very light of foot—hoof damage is immeasurably less than that arising from cows. Perhaps the most ingenious feature of deer as warring animals, however, is their appearance; for they have an additional and quite astonishingly effective protective device that is best described by its code name, the Bambi Factor. All deer look like Bambi and this affords them almost total invulnerability, no matter what they do to your garden.

After deer, the armoured enemy takes the form of hares, squirrels, rabbits, moles and assorted rodents, especially mice and voles. **Hares** are fairly uncommon as garden adversaries but can cause appreciable harm to young trees and shrubs by stripping the bark. **Rabbits**, by contrast, are quite exceptionally numerous and can cause a similar type of injury by bark stripping but in general are more significant as browsers of vegetation. They too have a form of protection somewhat similar to that utilised by deers, in this case the Peter Rabbit Effect, but it seems much less reliable until the creature is seen at very close quarters. Unlike the hare, which is a fairly solitary foe, the rabbit is gregarious. It occurs in squads, companies, battalions and sometimes entire regiments, all having a quite remarkable ability to replace troop losses very quickly indeed.

Squirrels are efficiency personified. They are fast moving, silent and especially adept at swinging upwards into the third dimension afforded by tree branches, either as a means of escape or of providing access to unconquered territory. They swoop down quickly to ground level, changing immediately from transport to attack modes, and dine on plant life both above and below soil level. By means of still secret location devices, crocus corms and lily bulbs can be detected with astonishing facility even when buried many centimetres below the surface. I feel that when a squirrel invasion is predicted, there is much to be said for evacuating tender young things to safe, non-wooded havens and for protecting such national treasures as *Lilium regale* by moving them into large containers kept close to base until the danger has passed.

The rodents comprise a largely unseen enemy, a large, nocturnal army of small, fast movers. Small they may be but in relation to their size, **wood mice** and **short-tailed voles** are as aggressive as any opposition our plants encounter. All manner of vegetation is nibbled and spoiled, but the greatest damage ensues when entry is effected to military stores containing apples, bulbs or corms. The numbers of mice and voles that gain entry to gardens is often only appreciated when traps are used and as many rodents caught as traps are put down. In some seasons, the vole militia in particular multiplies at a prodigious rate and takes on almost plague proportions—as many as 500 voles can occur per half-acre.

Deserving of a special category among the armoured brigade is the black peril: the lone, subterranean tunnelling machine that masquerades as the **mole**. There are those who would have you believe that the mole is a potentially harmless

The mole, a foe to count with the most sinister.

or even beneficial creature that goes to war by accident—that its undermining of defences and gardens in general is an incidental result of harmless civil engineering activity. Don't you believe it. The sheer directed malice with which a mole will make a bee-line for the finest area of turf in the neighbourhood is no accident; it is a deliberate ploy to destroy our resolve to fight by striking at the heart of what we all hold most dear, our lawns. And even when you consider that the mole's excuse for its destructive tunnelling is a search for food, this can engender little sympathy either. For the food of

A large dog can wreak havoc in a small garden.

the mole is one of ours: the earthworm that works day and night, year in and year out at the thankless task of mixing in organic matter to the soil and keeping the underground environment well aerated and healthy for plants' roots. Yet the worm's only reward for this devoted trail is to fall prey to that set of razor-sharp teeth. Don't be fooled by the propaganda; the mole is a foe to count with the most sinister.

I have left until last a strange mixture of heavy artillery, a group that is perhaps sound reason for considering every man (and woman, and garden) an island. Who can you trust in times of war when those that are superficially so similar to your own troops are in fact no more to be trusted than the common enemy from without? You may seem to have much to share with neighbouring gardeners when you discuss your triumphs and failures, your relative efficiency at excluding airborne and land-based invaders. Yet, turn your back and it could be his renegade, undisciplined army that directs its weapons at you, sometimes to complete neighbourly indifference. And how destructive they are, the neighbouring **cat**, **dog** and **small boy**. The damage they inflict is evil, wicked, mindless destruction of flower beds and a despoiling and fouling of your land. But there is almost no defence against them, no action that can be taken without bringing down the International Court upon your head. Truly they show that war is all-embracing; trust no one.

5   *Biological Weapons*

Mankind has always had an innate fear of the invisible. Being unable to see the cause of your anxiety was the stock in trade of Edgar Allan Poe, Alfred Hitchcock and their kind. And so it has been over the centuries when one nation has taken arms against another. But invisibility in warfare takes two rather different forms. The first represents the change from the ancient situation of two armies face to face, eyeball to eyeball, across the field of battle, to the ability to fire weapons from beyond the horizon. That change may have caused paroxysms of concern for our ancestors but is is now an accepted fact of warring life. The second and still less readily appreciated weapon is that which remains invisible even when it arrives. In garden warfare, I distinguish two rather different versions among them—the biological weaponry which is my concern in this chapter and those that constitute the germ warfare that I shall describe in the next.

Biological weapons are neither plant nor animal but belong to the third of the five great kingdoms of animate beings, the fungi. Fungi are universal in occurrence and there is scarcely an environment on earth that one or other species has not colonised. They are also extremely numerous and extremely diverse—there are probably more species of fungi than of flowering plants in the world. And their diversity includes on the one hand species like the cultivated mushroom that are undeniably on our side and on the other, **honey fungus** and the causes of **clubroot** and **blackspot** that undeniably are not. Fungi are admirably equipped as adversaries for any garden, for by their very nature, they are unable to manufacture their own food in the fashion of green plants. Their nutrients must come therefore from other organisms.

Nonetheless, many fungal species, including the cultivated mushroom, are very useful allies in feeding solely on dead plant remains and generally filling the role of the undertakers and sanitary operators of garden society. But among the fungal ranks are many that feed not on dead but on living plants, some having developed sophisticated life sucking structures that enable them to continue feeding and growing whilst their unfortunate victim remains alive, its own bodily resources channelled into the demands of the parasite. When this gruesome life form is coupled with an invisible transport system, the significance and effectiveness of the fungal weapon can be appreciated to the full.

For fungi form not seeds but spores, microscopic reproductive structures that are produced in quite prodigious quantity—a single **honey fungus** toadstool, for instance, may liberate ten million million spores within a few days. Almost all spores produced above ground are dispersed by the wind and nothing, but nothing, can stop them from arriving in your garden. You can neither see them nor smell them (although on occasion, hay-fever sufferers may sneeze from

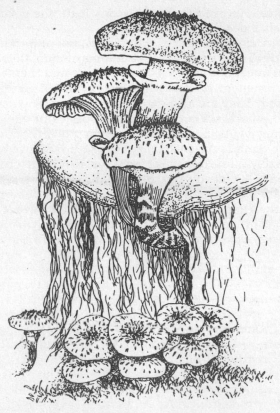

A single honey fungus toadstool may liberate ten million million spores in a few days.

them). There is no known radar or telescope that can spot
them, no barrage balloon, hedge, fence or barbed wire that
can keep them out. Only in the field of agriculture has anyone
devised anything approaching an early warning system—the
Beaumont scheme works on the indirect principle of knowing
the climatic conditions conducive to the release of the spores
of the potato blight fungus and advises farming vigilantes to

take up their weapons when the appropriate combination of conditions has occurred.

But for all other fungal weaponry, the only signs of an attack appear when it has succeeded—when the invisible spores have landed on their targets, germinated and infected the defenceless plant. For this is the outward manifestation of the most subtle aspect of the fungus as an enemy. It is by its very nature self-perpetuating and is only revealed when it has set up an advance base and begun to proliferate within the heart of your territory. For although spores may shower down in countless thousands from the air, it matters not that all but one drop harmlessly into the soil. That one, arriving on a susceptible plant, will be perfectly adequate to start afresh the whole process, but with the significant advantage that the additional spores that it produces in turn will now have only a very short distance to travel before reaching more

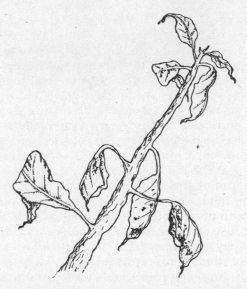

Despite the damage, it is hard not to admire the sophisticated target selection of mildew.

target plants. Hence their chances of success are so much greater and the single spear-head attack can soon become an all-swamping invasion.

There is a further, rather important feature of the spore and the fungal weapon in general; they are produced with varying degrees of sophisticated target selection device. Some, like the **grey mould** *Botrytis*, are crude, almost totally non-discriminatory weapons, attacking pretty well any type of vegetation on which they land. Raining down from above like unguided missiles, they attack the gentle, soft-hearted lettuce as well as the big, bustling, bristly pumpkin and so crude are they that an attack is as likely to develop on their own allies, the weed plants, as it is on our charges. *Botrytis* is in fact a thoroughly untrustworthy customer for it is quite likely to masquerade as a friend, at one minute browsing away placidly on the compost heap graveyard and at the next, when your back is turned, leaping with a bound through the greenhouse window, to alight on some somnolent tomato, contentedly gorged with water and potash. The utterly defenceless salad then scarcely has time to twitch its bracts before it is reduced to a lifeless, gory pulp.

At the opposite extreme from the simple lumbering grey mould terror weapon lies a group of enemies and weapons for which it is hard not to have considerable technical admiration. Some of the **mildews** and even more especially some of the **rust** fungi have such sophisticated target selection mechanisms that they can single out for attack a specific variety of a specific plant and leave the surrounding civilian population unharmed. And at the same time, many of these weapons conduct a gentleman's war, adhering to rules of fair play. For whilst they can proliferate within a season or so of an initial attack and cause considerable damage among the indigenous population, they make life particularly difficult for themselves in respect of their long-term survival. They require the proximity of another, unrelated target plant to be able to complete fully their life cycles, and as they make well known

39

the identity of this plant, they thus offer to the thinking gardener at least a modicum of hope for the future.

In a rather special league among biological weaponry are the subterranean varieties. Whilst most fungal spores land on or in the soil at some stage of their lives, others live there permanently, never showing their heads above the surface. They only make known the fact that they have been smuggled into the garden when your plants begin to show indications of ailing. Then, as the plants are lifted carefully for examination by a field surgeon prior to transportation to the greenhouse hospital, it is seen that far from being the carefree, foot-loose soldiery that you knew and loved, they are actually foot-less. The wretched underground enemy has devoured each plant's root system, leaving them with not a leg to stand on.

The means by which injury is caused to plants by fungal weapons are many and varied and I have touched on some of them already. Most of the underground attacks result, as with **damping off**, in root death or even, as with **clubroot**, in a hideous malformation, later to become septic and gangrenous. Above ground, no part of the plant is immune—buds, flowers and fruits may succumb to rot and disfigurement, while leaves will become variously spotted and may actually drop

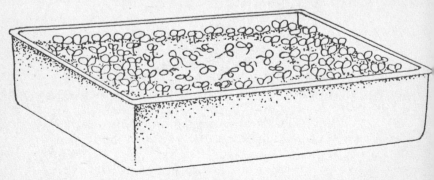

Damping off, the dreaded underground enemy that devours a seedling's root system.

off prematurely. Young stems may soften and weaken or their water conducting elements may be blocked, leading to the upper parts being starved of water and wilting. Larger, older, woody stems may become cankered, developing grotesque, blister-like lesions as the invading fungus effects a slow strangulation. There is almost no limit to the nastiness that can be inflicted by one organism upon another. The most fiendish plots devised in the course of human warfare have nothing on the fungus and plant struggle that is enacted before our very eyes every day that we garden.

6   Germ Warfare

Biological weapons are bad enough but germ weapons are even worse. For whilst fungal spores are certainly invisible, they germinate and usually reveal themselves once their wicked work of infection is done. Then the delicate fluff of mould growth offers you certain knowledge of the cause of the injury even if it may also provide no guarantee that the poor afflicted being will ever recover. But the germ weapon begins as invisible and ends as invisible. You will never see it arrive, never see it at work and never see it go again; if indeed it ever does. Germ is a loose, group term for what, in more technical language, we should call bacteria and viruses, and it is the latter that provide far and away the biggest threat in terms of garden warfare.

A virus has been called a living, self-replicating chemical.

Certainly it bears no resemblance or relationship to any other organism. If the perfect weapon had to be devised, the virus must surely come close to filling that role. All are not only invisible to the naked eye, they are invisible to the naked microscope, too, and only with the technology of electron optics is it possible to reveal their form and structure. They have also been called perfect, complete parasites, for they live out their existences (I am reluctant to call them lives) entirely within the cells of their wretched victims and actually usurp the cells' function to their own ends. It is enforced, microscopic slavery, for the poor cell works its nucleus out simply to keep the virus alive.

Several questions must now present themselves. If viruses are wholly invisible, how can they ever be detected? If they are confined to the insides of their victims, how can they be transported to attack new areas? And if they are both invisible and internal, what hope can there be of ever putting up a defence against them? Of course, attack by viral weapons can only be confirmed when it has achieved its objective and the plants begin to suffer. One small crumb of comfort can be gleaned, however, from the fact that the effects that viruses have on their victims are generally uniquely distinctive The injuries for the most part are quite unlike those produced by other weapons and, in many ways, they are less gruesome. There are no gaping wounds, no oozing sap or broken limbs. None of the tissues decay or offer the hideous gangrenous spectacle that characterises so many types of fungal attack. Sometimes, there is a small degree of spotting of leaves and quite frequently a superficially rather attractive speckling and patterning in yellow or paler green shades, in contrast with the generally darker colour of the foliage. In fact, this yellow speckling is about as appealing as smallpox, for it reveals the presence of one or more of the most important types of virus weapon, the **mosaic**. In a few instances, dark coloured flowers actually assume a particularly endearing yellow or white streaking. This is an extremely

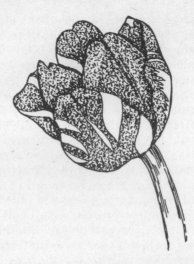

The telltale white stripes of tulip breaking virus, darling of Dutch flower painters.

subtle ploy on the part of the enemy, however, for it may actually encourage the unwitting gardener to propagate these plants at the expense of other, normal forms. Many an innocent cottage garden has become a haven for yellow flecked wallflowers that are in fact reservoirs of virus disease waiting its chance to strike deep into the heart of the vegetable plot. And in the seventeenth century, when warfare was not what it is today, Dutch flower artists, bless them, were actually duped into painting still-life vases of **striped tulips**, a subject almost as endearing as a canister of nerve gas.

Sometimes, the real horror of virus attack can be revealed more dramatically by the appearance of strange malformations and outgrowth—by the leaves of tomatoes taking on the semblance of fern leaves, for instance, or of pea leaves bearing small, tongue-like excrescences. But the most insidious feature of virus germ warfare is in its long-term effects. For a plant cannot shrug off virus infection in the way that appropriate treatment can mend the effects of fungal or pest attack. Perennial plants are afflicted for life and no matter how well they may be cared for by their loved ones, the old war wounds will return to plague them year after year, gradually sapping away their strength. Eventually, the weakness that the infection bestows may well become too much and they succumb to some everyday passing mould spore or aphid attack; an insignificant enough trouble that a healthy plant could have shrugged off easily.

Most frustrating of all, and in many ways most ghoulish, are those viruses that work so stealthily that many years may pass before you are even aware that your plants have been attacked. It is probably no exaggeration to say that a very high proportion of perennial, (especially woody) plants have been attacked at some time in the past and are now host to internal virus contamination. In consequence, they are smaller, less vigorous and bear fewer and smaller flowers and fruit than nature originally intended. Only now that it is possible artificially to cure such plants by prolonged and painstaking treatment in the plant hospitals of research laboratories can truly healthy specimens be obtained for comparison. These virus infected plants are living evidence of the continuing guerilla war being fought in your garden, even when you may have thought that you were actually living in a time of relative peace.

But as if the little-by-little wearing down of the strongest constitution were not enough, the virus weapon has one further particularly unpleasant twist to its nature. For once a plant is infected, the infection will very probably be passed on to its offspring, and so generation after generation will fall prey. This aspect of the disease is most serious in those plants that reproduce vegetatively—through the medium of bulbs, corms, tubers or rhizomes, for instance. Fortunately, those plants that have the wit to reproduce themselves by seeds are better protected, for relatively few viruses can pass from parent plant to offspring in this manner.

The pale yellow speckling of mosaic virus on a rose leaf.

But there remains the conundrum of how these night-marish weapons are delivered to their targets and of how they then travel within a garden from plant to plant. With yet another example of low cunning, viruses have coerced other creatures to give them a free ride. Clearly, before utilising the virus as a war weapon, the military planners sat around their table and looked carefully for all the free-living animals in the world that routinely gain access to the insides of plants, preferably without doing immediate irreparable damage themselves. And having browsed the zoological literature, their eyes not surprisingly lighted upon a group that I have already described in some detail in the account of airborne invaders—the sap suckers. What better delivery vehicles can there be for a germ weapon than a creature that is present in vast numbers, flies readily from one plant to others and inserts its feeding apparatus deeply into plant tissues? In our climate, it is principally **aphids** that have been entrusted with the task, yet another reason for viewing with anxiety the aerial hordes that descend from the great blue yonder as

46

soon as the chill of early spring gives way to the warm threat of summer. In other, warmer parts of the world, **whiteflies** and other sap-sucking insects have found themselves doubly damned through their involvement with the international virus trafficking fraternity.

Fortunately, I am at last able to offer you a little more comfort, for not all viruses are delivered quite so quickly or efficiently. Many of those that are specifically targeted against fruit trees, for instance, are borne not on the back nor in the guts of aphids but inside those other sap-sucking pests, **eelworms**. And of course, just as eelworms themselves tend to be fairly static opponents, so the viruses they carry remain very much where they are placed. I confess this is a two-edged sword (and a mixture of military metaphors) for you will recall my concern about any subterranean opponent—the soil is quite simply no medium in which to go to war. Whilst soil-borne viruses travel slowly, therefore, they do contaminate your land for a very long time with very little likelihood of their ever being eradicated. I hope, however, that I shall not leave you too gloomy and with too much foreboding about your prospects in the face of germ warfare. We can be cunning, too, and there are some exciting new counter-attack measures that I shall be explaining later.

7 The Quislings

There are two major ways of ensuring that your name becomes a neologism. You can try inventing something new, original and worthy—a motor car like Henry Ford, road surfacing like John McAdam or even fish-fingers like Clarence Birdseye. Alternatively, you can act in a manner that people are unlikely to forget. Thus, Captain C. C. Boycott who was shunned for his intransigence, or, most reprehensible of all, Major Vidkun Quisling who aided the enemy occupying his native land. There are quislings in all wars and the war of the garden is no exception, for we have several instances of plants that outstay their welcome, turn on their owners and, in extreme cases, become almost indistinguishable from weeds.

I have before me a gardening book of the early nineteenth century. In it is a description of a singularly appealing plant—a herbaceous perennial some three or four feet tall. It was apparently a fairly uncommon native species at the time, to be found only in rocky areas but very amenable to cultivation. This plant carried a spike of purple flowers and evidently was considered at least as attractive when producing its feathery seed capsules. Its appeal for gardeners was obvious and it was planted widely and greatly admired. But after relatively few seasons, its untrustworthy nature was revealed. Those feathery capsules produced seeds that germinated with consummate ease and were parachuted on the wind to all corners—beds, borders, rock gardens; nowhere escaped a landing. The young airborne troops grew quickly and rapidly subdued the less assertive inhabitants. In fact, after a very few years with no counter-attack the conquest could become total. Oh, yes, the name of this so thoughtfully recommended subject—it was *Epilobium angustifolium*, the **rosebay willowherb**.

In times gone by, another well-known plant was clasped to gardeners' embrace; or perhaps more accurately, to herb gardeners' embrace; and look where that has brought us. For it was called herb gerard, bishop weed or gout weed. Herb gerard was just a code word—the brazen presence of the undisguised name 'weed' should have alerted the innocent. Today we know it better as **ground elder** and a more persistent member of the occupying forces in our gardens would be very hard to find. But the ground elder story displays other aspects of the ingenuity that some of our enemies will employ. It is now extremely well entrenched not only in our gardens but amongst our native plants too, and appears to have camouflaged itself to the extent of actually being considered a member of the native flora. Even the most careful botanical observer is likely to be uncertain of its real status—our standard reference book on native plants lists it as'? Introduced. Said to have been introduced and cultivated as a pot-herb, now very well naturalised'. I am not so charitable. I have been in the garden warfare business too

Rosebay willowherb, the garden perennial that ran riot.

long to bother with question marks. This plant is a foreigner. It fooled someone (probably a mediaeval monk who was preoccupied at the time with higher things), into believing that it could cure his ailment. You can imagine the scene: the knock at the monastery door late one night. The incumbent abbot, Father Gerard, complete with gout, staggers from his work bench to be greeted by a complete stranger who assures him that his discomfort can be banished in return for a simple home. Nothing special was asked or expected—a humble border lodging with the parsley and the onions would suffice. Of course, no one could turn away such an offer; and within a matter of weeks, parsley, onions and almost everything else had vanished under a rampant green carpet. And here it is still, and here are we, six hundred years later, ruing the charity and gullibility of old man Gerard and his wretched gout.

Not content, however, with having won its way into our homes (although not our hearts), ground elder rubbed salt into the wound. It developed a different uniform—a rather attractive striped number, alternately green and white, which it called variegatum. And the propaganda machinery was set in full motion. Apologies were offered for the maltreatment of old Gerard, a reminder was issued that the thing really did cure gout and an assurance was put about that variegatum was a conscientious objector if not actually pacifist. Once again it was given a welcome, border room was given over to it and variegated ground elder was planted with care and admiration. Yet once again, off it went; a little slower perhaps, its aggression tempered slightly by its striped uniform, but an enemy nonetheless.

Lessons are truly learned the hard way in the horticultural world. Having given ground elder a free ticket to occupation, we then turned our attention to a sweet little thing from the Mediterranean. Someone should have noticed that it was a close relative of the stinging nettle. Someone should also have realised that not for nothing had it acquired the common

51

names of **mind-your-own-business** or **mother of thousands**. But no doubt the logic applied to it was that once applied to the Romans—that nothing from the sunny south could ever be truly at home in our northern climes. So *Helxine soleirolii* was taken north, carried across our borders, into our gardens and even into our homes. In fact, as a pot plant, confined and carefully watched, it can be a pleasant companion. But grown as far too many a gardening book still recommends, 'in cool, moist and shady places over rocks', its true character becomes all too apparent. It is a creep and has quite clearly been trained as a secret lawn subjugating weapon. Once in and amongst lawn turf it becomes an occupying force of great tenacity. And there it joins one of the great quislings of twentieth century gardening. Astonishingly, *Veronica filiformis*, the **creeping speedwell**, is still sometimes suggested as a garden plant, with, in one reference book, the modest caveat that it is 'apt to be invasive, colonising even among grass'. *Even* among grass must be the cry going up across the nation as lawns turn ever bluer year by year. The very turf itself appears to have been forced into wearing the invader's uniform and it is now almost too late to turn the tide. And like so many other quislings, the creeping speedwell has given up sex in favour of the alternative life-style of professional smotherer. Those blue flowers are just a cover for more sinister goings on for they are all but barren.

As the years roll by, so we learn to be a little more circumspect over choosing our friends and it is hard to imagine that another rosebay willowherb, ground elder or creeping speedwell could trick its way into our affections. But in saying this, there are those on whom a careful watch must still be kept. Look at the **weeping willow** that so literally undermines the very foundations of our civilisation. And I can think of several other garden inhabitants that may wear our colours yet behave sufficiently arrogantly to warrant our suspicion. Take the boys and the girls in blue for a start. And in particular, cast your eye over a pair that have not even attempted to disguise their far-flung origins by changing their names. I have no hesitation in saying that, like *Veronica*, both *Campanula portenschlagiana* and *Campanula poscharskyana* are creeps. In the manner of war-weary soldiers the world over, they hang around garden corners and over garden walls, quite

The weeping willow will literally undermine the foundations of our civilisation.

decorative in their way. It is only when you watch them closely, week by week, that you come to realise they are not languid at all but down and out fifth columnists. Each time your back is turned, they take a step towards the honest residents but do this so stealthily that you scarcely notice until it is too late. In my own garden an innocent and much-loved *Hebe pagei* was completely overwhelmed by a creeping campanula without my noticing it. By then it was too late; the once healthy form was little more than a living corpse and there was nothing more to do than consign it to the great compost heap in the sky.

And there is a big foreign bully in my herbaceous border, too. I keep it contained by annual hard work for I admire its appealing roughness. But I know that given half a chance, half a season to be precise, gardener's garters, *Phalaris arundinacea* var. *picta*, will respond to the pleadings of its masters in the nearby fields and romp away, across the gentle irises, over the

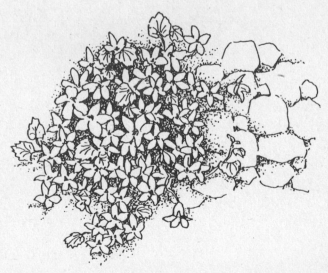

I have no hesitation in calling Campanula portenschlagiana *a creep.*

serenely browsing *Meconopsis* and trample under its wiry rhizomes all manner of tiny botanical treasures. Yes, I am afraid that even devoted friends like *Geranium* 'Claridge Druce' can be swayed when they catch a glimpse over your garden boundaries and see relatives living beyond the wooden curtain. *Geranium robertianum* beckons alluringly. Life looks so good from this side of the border that our garden friends are impelled to grow at a prodigious pace and produce innumerable offspring in their endeavour to reach this apparently promised land out there in the fields and woods. If only they knew; if only they realised that it is a land of foul and noxious chemicals, a territory where cows trample unrestrained and where squirrels and rabbits have free tickets to pillage. The proverbial grass may seem so much greener over there but like many misguided idealists before them, it is only after crossing the frontier that they discover the dreadful truth.

8 Natural Hazards

There are countless examples throughout history of armies being defeated and battles or even entire wars being lost, not through the actions of skilled defenders or the effectiveness of good intelligence, but simply through nature having its way. Napoleon, Alexander the Great and the Duke of Medina Sidonia all learned that, in different ways, there are some things over which even the cleverest of commanders can exercise no control. Garden warfare is no different and, just as in real warfare, the effects can be manifest in several ways. Our gardening activities can come grievously undone because there are topographical or soil features of the garden that create problems, because we attempt to undertake a major campaign such as planting at an inappropriate time of the year, because the weather takes a sudden and unexpected change, or simply because we are expecting our troops to survive in a climate that is totally different from those of their native lands.

The benefits and disadvantages that the **position of the site** confers are perhaps the most frequently unappreciated hazards. The geographical location of a garden has a major bearing on how cold it will become. Whilst cabbage palms may grow contentedly through the mild winters of the Scilly Isles, they will have a very rude shock in the Scottish Highlands almost before the month of July is through. Although there are one or two notable exceptions, plants, like all other troops, will generally succeed best in a climate as similar as possible to that of their homelands. There are the odd

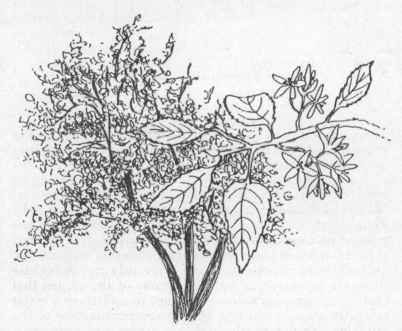

Amelanchier lamarckii *can bend without harm before the strongest, coldest breeze.*

horticultural Gurkhas such as pot marigolds that will succeed almost anywhere but unfortunately, unlike the Gurkhas, these tend to be on the Other Side.

There are nonetheless relatively few plants, even those from the warmest climes, that don't appreciate the opportunity for a short spell in the great campaign outdoors. They may by their nature be urban guerillas, much more at home fighting the hazards of creeping central heating and stifling dry air than the crawling and flying invaders outside, but a change is as good as a rest and they can be given leave of absence from these onerous duties for a few months during the summer. Then, the heat of the central heating struggle is off and a posting to an undemanding sentry duty in the cool shade of the peat bed will be more than welcome. A healthy diet of fresh water and potash, a refreshing shower of real rain, and they can return again in the autumn, rejuvenated and ready to take on the worst that the all-demanding, executive, semi-detached, G-plan world can throw at them.

Then there are those plants that cannot tolerate **exposure**. Perhaps I should qualify this, for in common with many people of my acquaintance, exposure to the sun is usually acceptable whereas exposure to a cold wind is not. That apparently robust creature, the paeony, can be most unhappy in a buffeting gale whereas the seemingly frail pea tree and the amelanchier can bend without harm before the strongest, coldest breeze. Nonetheless, physical size may be no measure of robustness, and in a really strong gale, the bigger they are, the harder they fall. There are, however, some harmless, helpless garden residents for whose welfare and future it seems all the fighting is done and the war is waged. That gentlest of garden inhabitants, the cut-leaved maple, is a classic example in this category, for its particularly tender skin will not stand a great deal of exposure to anything and it even prefers a modicum of shade in summer.

Napoleon is supposed to have maintained that his army marched on its stomach. If he did, he was probably right, and

In a really strong gale, the bigger they are, the harder they fall.

in garden warfare there is no doubt that the armies march on their root hairs. But these root hairs must have access to the appropriate **nutrients** if they are to function efficiently. No doubt there are historical analogies for plants failing to grow in incorrect soil—I am sure, for instance, that Scots Chieftains have rued having to force-feed their men with roast beef in times of hardship, just as the Grenadiers must on occasion have foundered on a diet of porridge. It is no different from expecting a rhododendron or a camellia to give of their best when their feeding bowls are filled with lumps of limestone. And anyone who has seen roses perform in a deep, moisture-retentive clayey loam must inevitably feel only guilt at sending them into the struggle on a diet of thin, free-draining sand.

But there is more to the soil than merely the offer of a supply of rations. It can be heavy or light, wet or dry, and I cannot over-emphasise the importance of using the appro-

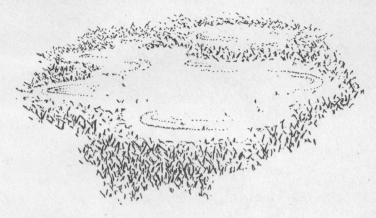

Heavy, wet conditions can result in large puddles on a sodden lawn.

priate regiment for each set of conditions. A light, sandy soil is the home of the horticultural camel corps—the succulents like houseleeks that, unlike proper camels, really do store water in their humps. And the lightweight, fast growing species of pinks and carnations that almost seem to skim over the soil's surface are at home here, too. In wetter, heavier conditions come wetter, heavier plants—really tough, self-opinionated marines in the shape of American lysichitons and Japanese irises. But once you actually reach open water, all will be well for the navy's here. And although in most gardens, the Senior Service makes only a modest appearance, the elite nymphaea troops will grace and defend any pool against all comers, the carrier launched water-lily beetle being virtually alone in finding a chink in their armour plating. Largely unseen, of course, but never to be forgotten, are the submariners, the buccaneering Canadian pondweed and smooth, unruffled myriophyllum that cruise below the water surface, ensuring that the water stays clean and healthy for its other residents.

I have not analysed battlefield successes in relation to the time of year in which they were fought but I have made long

A raw young coniferous recruit should not be expected to face his first adventures in the front line during the winter.

and careful study of the great campaigns of gardening warfare on a month by month basis. Clearly, there are winter troops and summer troops. I would be most reluctant to expect a raw young coniferous recruit to face his first adventures at the front during the winter. His outdoor clothing is untried, fresh from the store and likely to abrade and chafe—one of the disadvantages of such soldiery being issued with a single, all-year uniform. Only a well battle-hardened conifer would I reckon at all safe—and even then, I would prefer to offer the additional protection of an armour screen. But a deciduous warrior is a different matter. He has the common sense to abandon his lightweight summer wear as soon as the chill winds of autumn begin to blow and I would have no compunction about letting him win his spurs either then or in the early spring. Winter really does search out the true grit of any plant and so often it is a matter of proper conditioning.

In genuinely cold climates, there is much to be said for restricting your choice to the real Polar brigades. Alpines, for instance, whose natural home is the wind- and snow-swept mountain top or even the fringes of the Tundra itself, will welcome the posting to a British winter, although even this may not be quite to their liking. For the British seasons are not all that these immigrants might expect. Take what is ostensibly one of the toughest customers you could wish to have on your side, a deciduous conifer from the frozen north of Russia called the Siberian larch. Time and again, well-meaning commanding officers have brought these fighting plants to strengthen their British gardens; and time and again they have failed. Hardly ever has the Siberian larch proved its real worth here, and they have finished up being crippled and pensioned off, or even, in the less charitable regiments, dismissed the service with ignominy. Poor plants, so ill-prepared for our fits and starts seasons where winter never knows when to end. A few fine, bright days in February and they have taken out their summer uniforms and marched forth, full of hope for campaigning in the warm spring to come. But how badly they have judged the climate, for as like as not, within a few days, back comes winter, back come frosts and their thin summer garb proves no protection at all.

9   The Secret Weapon

Every war produces its surprises. At the onset of hostilities, there can be no knowing what inventions old mother necessity will throw up. The First World War produced the tank, the Second, radar. Warfare in the garden follows the trend too and the novice gardener taking up arms for the first time against the hostile hordes waiting on his every move will soon learn this. There are of course the many fairly obvious forces that I have described already, most of them rendered visible sooner or later and most of them reasonably predictable to anyone who has seen other gardens or given the subject more than a fleeting thought. It is only when you are actually embroiled in the heat of the struggle that a disturbing truth gradually begins to dawn. Among the things that go wrong with your troops are several for which there can be no obvious explanation. No pieces of tissue disappear from leaves with only teeth or beak marks to betray their destinations. No gradually increasing infestations of airborne aphids swamp tender young shoots and there is no obvious leaf-to-leaf fighting between your loved ones and passing renegade groundsel detachments. What happens is quite simply that everything begins to look one degree under. Growth and vitality are not what they should be; leaves are smaller, flower smaller and fewer, fruit less tasty and vegetables tough.

In time, many such afflicted plants gradually take on curious but still far from explicable symptoms—strange black blotches, small patches of dead tissue, even irregularly mottled leaf patterns of light and dark. When the novice gardener begins to think a little more deeply, talks to his allies over the fence or even consults standard manuals of gardening militarism, he may be forgiven for thinking that germ warfare has begun. Some of the effects afflicting his vegetation seem to fit the description of virus attack but on reading more deeply it will become apparent that all does not quite tally. There are the wrong symptoms on the wrong plants, the wrong combination of symptoms on the right plants, or even the wrong disposition of the effects across the bed or plot. Why, for instance, should all the lettuce plants on one side of a bed be affected severely with a pale leaf mottle which diminishes gradually from plant to plant as the opposite side is approached? Surely no virus germ weapon can be injected in quite such a carefully orchestrated manner. No, indeed not. The explanation is more enigmatic still: the enemy has employed a secret weapon to bring about your downfall.

Ultimately, the secret weapon almost invariably achieves its results through starvation. Your plants are being denied some vital food resource, but rather than adopting the sledgehammer approach of hijacking a fertiliser delivery lorry or dynamiting your compost heap, the enemy's modus

operandi has been more subtle. You would notice very
quickly if all foodstuffs were withheld simultaneously,
whereas the little by little approach can have serious effects
before you realise what is happening. For any army needs a
balanced diet: a careful blend of **nitrogen**, **phosphate** and
potash as its main course at each meal, but an equally
important tonic of other substances, too—**calcium**, **mag-
nesium**, **iron** and **boron**, for example. Rather as old-time
seafarers suffered scurvy when denied Vitamin C, so garden
plants cannot give of their best without all these individual
elements. A shortage of nitrogen, phosphate or potash can
sometimes be used to catch out the really unwary gardener,
but these effects are rather too obvious to fool the experienced
who can, however, come to grief when trace nutrients are in
short supply.

In most instances, it is through the well-tried propaganda
technique of disinformation that the secret weapon achieves

Lime induced chlorosis is one of the most widespread effects of the secret weapon.

its objectives. Much gardening literature simply does not contain details of the early detection and treatment of nutritional deficiencies and often implies that germ warfare is their cause; I can only surmise that editors and gardening writers must have been brainwashed not to include the requisite facts. An alternative hypothesis is that the gardening press is actually controlled by enemy agents who deliberately edit out the necessary details, but this is a possibility so appalling that I prefer not to entertain it until I have undertaken a careful examination of the appropriate Ministry of Agriculture Minutes in thirty years' time. At least there is the assurance that if you are reading these words now, one free press must still be functioning to bring the truth to the oppressed horticulturists of the world. My word processor will not be stilled by foreign agents, and although these lines must perforce be printed in invisible onion juice ink and borne by carrier pigeon to a secret printing works, I shall have the satisfaction of knowing that the long-banned words can at last be read by gardeners everywhere. Neither High Court Injunction nor lethal umbrella handle can stop me from writing 'blossom end rot', 'lime-induced chlorosis', 'black heart', 'marsh spot', 'tip burn', 'bitter pit', 'glassiness', 'cavity spot', 'internal browning', 'raan' or 'corky pit'. I don't even draw back from an expression so sensitive that even in times of peace, it has been uttered only in hushed tones between gardeners in shabby raincoats meeting after dusk at allotment corners. For the first time in the recent history of civilised western gardening and possibly the only time since the Restoration of the Royal Horticultural Society, I shall say 'whip-tail'.

Yes, the tragedy of the effects brought about by the secret weapon of gardening warfare is that their cause is so obvious when you know, so simple to avoid had you been told. The dreaded **lime-induced chlorosis** is perhaps at the same time the most serious and most widespread and yet the easiest to combat. For so many plants when grown on lime-rich soils are denied by simple soil chemistry the ability to take up many of the nutrients they require. And most important among these nutrients is the element iron, an essential component of the process by which green chlorophyll is made. In the absence of chlorophyll, plants turn a sickly, jaundiced yellow and are unable to function properly and do battle with the opposing forces, because this in turn means that they cannot correctly photosynthesise.

By contrast, a whole clutch of sickening injuries is brought about when plants are grown in conditions too acidic; when they are actually denied the calcium that they all require. Just as advertisements used to tell us of the importance of milk for babies in order that the calcium it contains could 'promote strong bones and teeth', so baby plant leaves and shoots have a comparable need for the same element. In the absence of sufficient calcium (and sometimes in the associated absence of boron), tender young parts blacken and shrivel to produce such effects as black heart in celery, internal browning in Brussels sprouts, bitter pit in apples, cavity spot in carrots and, commonest and most widely damaging of all, **blossom end rot** of tomatoes. I often feel that the poor innocent tomato is a victim of so much hardship in the garden generally that it seems grossly unfair that it should fall victim to much of the battleground weaponry too. There is good reason for

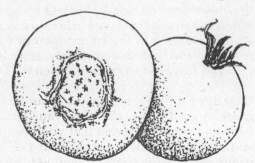

Most widely damaging of all, blossom end rot of tomatoes.

believing it the most ill-treated of all our own troops and in some regiments it is considered as little better than a slave. Brought here from its warm, South American home, it has been subjected to all manner of indignities. Sometimes it is made to grow outdoors in all the rigours and hardships of the British summer, force-fed with potash and expected to produce red, succulent fruit in the most inclement of conditions. Other tomatoes are locked up in greenhouses, confined in growing bags, tied to stakes, stripped of their side-shoots and then cursed when they fall short in their productiveness of the expectations engendered by some obscene illustration in that most pornographic of publications, the seed catalogue. So it is a sad irony that it is they who most frequently fall prey to gardening warfare's secret weapon.

PART TWO
DEFENCE AND COUNTER-ATTACK

1 Chemical Defence

There is some justification for believing that in only one respect does garden warfare differ from the real thing. By and large, the destructive power of dynamite and similar explosives finds little application in horticulture. The satisfaction of having rid your cabbage plot of caterpillars could be relatively small compensation for the ten-metre crater that takes its place in the middle of your garden. I admit, however, that there are occasions when the enemy does not seem to adhere to the same rules of engagement, and living through a low-level bombing raid by a squadron of De Havilland Wood Pigeons is an experience not to be dismissed lightly. But whatever the provocation, there can be no grounds for using the hand grenade in defence. (And curiously enough, wood pigeons and all other birds actually occupy a unique position

71

in global confrontation and enjoy legal protection. They have a genuine 007 brief of being licensed to kill innocent vegetation, but then have recourse to the International Court of Justice if retribution follows).

One of the stock defences against garden enemies has long been the chemical weapon and this has become so much a part of most gardeners' armouries that I am afraid it is a weapon they tend to use in preference to any other. This is a course of action that I deprecate. It is a symptom of civilisation lowering itself to the enemy's level—just because the Romans had spikes on their chariot wheels was no justification for Boadicea doing the same. But chemical weaponry does deserve some careful attention, for there is a very considerable range in unpleasantness displayed by garden chemicals, and at the more acceptable end of the spectrum are substances that we all enjoy as part of our daily diets and yet which can, on appropriate occasions, be deadly in their effects. Even among the substances that are distinctly inedible, there are many whose peripheral effects on the civilian population are not always properly appreciated. But at the other extreme are substances that, having obliterated the foe, then contaminate the soil for ages, with the result that instead of a garden fit for heroes, you have a garden fit for nothing. And whilst most gardeners realise that certain chemical defences are appropriate only against certain kinds of enemy (**pesticides** against pests, **fungicides** against fungi and **weedkillers** against weeds), is often not appreciated that within these groups of substance are materials that act more specifically—some fungicides only control certain types of fungi, for example.

Because they are so different in their effects, I shall say a little about anti-fungal, anti-pest and anti-weed weapons in turn. There are two principal ways in which the fungicidal weapon can be used; and the method required dictates the choice of substance. If the international outlook is bleak, world peace conferences have failed and war seems imminent, there can be some justification for erecting a chemical defence system. The first sign to be aware of is the onset of prolonged wet weather, for it is in such conditions that many biological weapons are deployed. When such weather occurs early in the season following a year in which serious attacks were

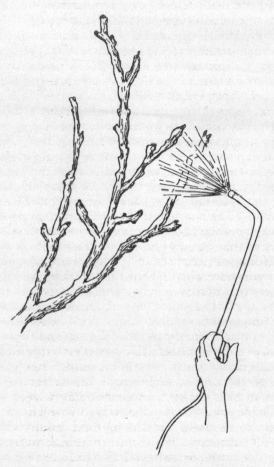

A protective winter spray is one justified use of chemical defence.

experienced, the portents are especially ominous. For no matter how effectively the previous assault has been repulsed, some 'sleepers' will almost certainly remain to renew the campaign from within your garden and add their impact to that of the newcomers arriving from without. The docile, none too intelligent potato often falls prey to just such an attack from the blight fungus and is one of the most important plants for which a **protective spray** (with a copper-containing fungicide, for instance) is justified. Usually, however, biological attacks occur rather less predictably and injuries have been inflicted before you realise what is happening. This is where a **systemic chemical** response is called for. A systemic chemical is absorbed into the body of the plant and offers protection from within—rather like government issue cod liver oil. It can seek out fungal growth even fairly well entrenched in the tissues, but a systemic fungicide, like **benomyl, carbendazim** or **thiophanate-methyl**, has other merits, too. Many of them tend to be intrinsically pretty good fungicides with effectiveness against a wide range of types of biological weapon. They are also invaluable in the hands of the inexperienced conscript. A protective fungicide like the copper-containing **Bordeaux Mixture** is only active where it lands—any parts of the plant that are missed remain unprotected, so they are of real effectiveness only when used by a trained marksman. A systemic substance can be aimed fairly inaccurately and yet still be operative over the whole plant as it is moved uniformly within its tissues.

Insecticides are usually divided into systemic and contact, the two categories having some of the same characteristics as systemic and protectant fungicides. A **systemic insecticide** is absorbed into the sap and is thus not only spread uniformly within the tissues but is actually present within the very substance on which sap-sucking pests feed. It provides a very special advantage in the combating of aerially invading suckers therefore. A **contact insecticide**, however, is not usually applied like a fungicide in a purely protective capacity.

It is used primarily against an enemy such as a caterpillar that is clearly conspicuous on the plant surface, although these chemicals may require almost sniper-like precision if they are to reach their targets. And when the pest is cunning enough to tuck itself away beneath leaves or even, like the leaf-rolling sawfly, to wrap them around itself, the pesticide will drip off quite harmlessly. It is generally true that most insecticides will control most insect pests, but one chemical is especially valuable in leaving the civilian population unharmed while eliminating aphids. It is called **pirimicarb** and is used by at least one armaments manufacturer in a weapon that combines it with a fungicide to give all-round protection to some of the most important groups in garden society, especially that well-known aristocratic family, the Roses.

One major drawback both with systemic fungicides and with systemic insecticides is that they can make you wait for your meal. Because they are absorbed within plant tissues and thus take some time to dissipate, a minimum interval (sometimes as much as two weeks) must elapse after treatment before edible plants can be eaten. In these circumstances, a protectant or contact product and a well-trained troop of marksmen may be a wiser course. In fact, in the kitchen garden, it may even be sensible to allow the enemy some modest gains with no chemical defence at all, simply luring him into a false sense of security and then launching a guerilla response.

But I mentioned earlier the possibility of pressing your own troops' rations into action as weapons, and the two chemicals that I have in mind could both be filched from the mess-room table. **Sodium chloride**, common salt, is an excellent weapon against the slug menace, and **hydrogen oxide** (or, to give it its more familiar name, water) can be directed forcibly through the gardening equivalent of a water cannon and very effectively break up rioting aphids.

To remove occupying weed forces requires a rather different type of chemical weapon, but this is an area where the armaments factories have been especially effective in devising new and sophisticated defences. Whilst there are sledgehammer weapons such as **paraquat** that kill everything they touch, they are generally used against small seedling weeds and in many of these instances a direct physical counter-assault with a hoe is more valuable and safer. But with the really well entrenched occupying forces, a chemical response is almost essential. The **systemic weedkillers** such as **glyphosate** and **alloxydim-sodium** will root out the most stubborn bindweed or couch grass, although as with nerve and tear gases, they must be used with care and preferably not on a windy day or they will blow back in the defenders' faces and eradicate their own forces. But perhaps the most

Selective lawn weedkiller is one of the most astonishing of all modern chemical weapons.

astonishing of all modern chemical weapons are the **selective lawn weedkillers**. I have mentioned earlier the special role that a lawn plays in any gardening war. It is the nerve centre of our entire domain and protection of the lawn against invasion is for many gardeners what garden warfare is all about. These selective chemicals are so ingenious that they can eradicate weeds that have been bold and brazen enough to take up residence within the lawn itself, in full view of the Parliament building (or kitchen window as it is more generally known).

Yes, I am afraid that chemical weapons are here to stay, and attempts at banning them by international treaty have so far failed. The Geneva talks have certainly resulted in a reduction in the range of substances used and the most noxious have been removed. Even so, suspicion remains that the stockpiles themselves may not have been disposed of—verification is quite exceptionally hard to introduce and the hawks among the agrochemical manufacturers have used their veto most effectively. Nonetheless, it is the responsibility of every civilised gardener to use chemical defences with the greatest circumspection and always to consider them the last, not the first recourse if the enemy is sighted.

2   Guerilla Warfare

'Set a thief to catch a thief' is an adage as old as gardening. Whilst the actual employment of thieves on your behalf may be a less than wise tactic, there is no doubt that there are occasions when every army, overtly or covertly, finds itself benefiting from a battalion or two of mercenaries. There are many precedents in real warfare for armies importing foreign troops to fight on their behalf against an enemy whose natural home is similar to their own. And there are many precedents, too, for an army that is fighting a war in an ally's territory to seek whatever means are at its disposal to encourage the local populace to harry an occupying common foe. Gardening is no different and there may be occasions when persuading your allies to go underground in order to defend themselves may almost be taken literally.

Before suggesting that you go to the considerable expense of flying in a specially trained counter-insurgency unit, allow me to consider the local inhabitants most likely to respond to a call to arms. Some of them are already very well known to most battling gardeners, even if they are generally unaware of how to organise a recruitment campaign. Best known of all are the most conspicuous: those beautifully elegant amazons known as **ladybirds**, troops who not only wear classically traditional uniforms reputedly designed by Balmain, but who have even had popular songs written about them. (It is with slight reluctance that I have to reveal nonetheless one of the best kept secrets in the history of warfare. Far be it from me to stoop to the lower reaches of the tabloid press, but to avoid

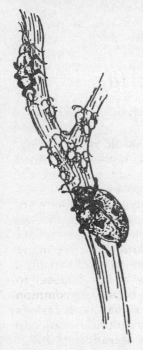

Ladybird larvae will devour greenfly with a prodigious appetite.

any possible embarrassment at mess-room parties, I feel it my duty to disclose that, despite their perfumed finery, at least half of all ladybirds are actually male.) Ladybirds do in fact have a juvenile larval fighting unit and it is they, rather than their elegant parents, that do the hard work, the more senior insects preferring not to soil their clothing with such basic adolescent activities as eating aphids. But what an appetite these teenagers have, each being perfectly capable of devouring up to five hundred greenfly during the course of their three weeks' development.

Almost as well known as the ladybird brigade is another conspicuously uniformed outfit. These, too, are airborne and are probably the finest exponents of helicopter tactics you are ever likely to see. So effective are they at standing still in mid-air that they have even been given the name **hover-flies**. Once again, it is not the adults but their voracious offspring that are most likely to respond to a 'Your garden needs you' appeal. Their aphid consumption, however, is greater even than that of ladybabies and, during their active working life, each hover-fly larva may devour one thousand pests, be they green, black or even grey in colour. Indeed, one member of this group, obviously with an eye to the immortality of an entry in the Guinness Book of Garden Warfare Records, was once observed to consume twenty-five aphids in as many minutes.

There are many larger creatures that need little persuading to induce them to take to a diet of the common insect enemy. That most endearing and efficient of armoured fighting machines, the **hedgehog**, is always willing to please and whilst, like frogs and insectivorous birds, its powers of discriminating between friend and foe are limited, its assistance is invaluable. In encouraging the local bird population, however, one must always be slightly careful. The bird table really is very often the northern convoy of garden warfare, providing sustenance for an ally to aid the fight against a common enemy, but in all honesty, it is an ally that cannot always be trusted and that has been known to turn its attention against your own troops on occasion. Even the aquatic environment can play its part in keeping pests in proportion. When the invasion comes, no stone must be left unturned in our search for help, and large goldfish submarines can sometimes be induced to surface and gulp in the odd crash-landed troops before they can take to their life rafts.

In a rather special league of guerilla fighters are those eight-legged wonders, **spiders**. For puzzling yet traditional reasons they have never achieved widespread popularity and are most unceremoniously turned away from post-battle victory parades around the bathroom. Yet they have brought guerilla tactics to a fine art and have perfected snaring traps without equal in the history of combat. Allow me this opportunity to launch a special campaign to change public opinion. If you can leave this chapter with an intention to love spiders a little more than you have ever done before, I shall have achieved one worthwhile objective.

Not only the insect enemy can fall prey to a well-organised guerilla campaign. Among the most tricky of the infiltrating enemies with which we have to contend are mites, many of which are so small that they pass unnoticed across our frontiers and then adopt guerilla tactics of their own, lying in wait unseen in nooks and crannies to strike out against unsuspecting vegetation. Very often they attack the more defenceless members of our population, in particular plants from foreign climates that have barely recovered after the trauma of a journey from the supermarket to the living room window ledge. Indoors, mites are very difficult to combat, having assumed an almost total and arrogant disregard for chemical defence systems. In the garden or greenhouse, however, they are more vulnerable. For outdoors, they are likely to come up against **bugs**—either of the **capsid** or **anthocorid** variety. These greatly unconsidered allies take a singular delight in dining on red spider mites, and among capsids in particular there are some astonishingly effective

81

counter-mite agents. I am reliably informed that there are individual bugs who have proudly painted over four thousand notches on their mandibles following distinguished careers in miticidal activity. In fact, a very few have actually been awarded the Gorge Cross for their heroism.

What can be done to aid the recruitment of our indigenous allies? Quite the simplest and most important operation is to employ no defence system that is unable to discriminate between them and the real enemy. When chemical defence is used, this is of course, extremely difficult, but I would remind you of the substance that I mentioned in the last chapter, **pirimicarb**. This is by no means the ideal chemical weapon, for if used on edible crops, at least two weeks must elapse between treatment and consumption. But pirimicarb does have the great merit of selectivity towards aphids, leaving other insects quite unharmed.

So far I have dwelt on the value of recruitment of local defence forces, but sometimes these campaigns have only limited effectiveness and some other system must be employed. For those gardeners determined to use guerilla warfare to its utmost, however, and provided the problem of invasion is confined to the greenhouse, there is always the option of bringing in the SAS. This now familiar abbreviation has its origin in the South American Spider system used to provide quick elimination of red spider mite infestation in greenhouses. The actual fighting unit is a creature called *Phytoseiulus persimilis*, another species of mite which has been brought over from its native land, trained in the ways of British greenhouses and is now available as small, mercenary groups that can be bought by interested gardeners. Unfortunately, there is a limit to the value of these tiny troopers as, with kamikaze-like disregard for their own future survival, they dine on red spider mites until all are eaten—and then inevitably die out themselves, being unable to make use of alternative rations. In a similar manner, the parasitic wasp-like creature, *Encarsia formosa*, will make short shrift of whitefly infestation in a greenhouse but suffers the additional drawback of rendering impossible any direct chemical defence against, for instance, aphids. For being insects themselves, encarsias will fall foul of the same weaponry.

Here lie the bodies of our gallant troops

3   Trench Warfare

The longer I do battle in my garden, the more I am convinced of the truth contained in the old adage about the answer lying in the soil. It is the soil over which or through which invading forces pass, and it is very often on or in the soil that defensive weapons are employed. Yet it is a difficult and intransigent medium in many ways—there is quite simply so much of it, and we find it very difficult to see a way through it all. But as well as the route by which many enemy forces come, it is also the source of much that is good for our own plant folk. With their roots anchoring them pretty firmly to one spot, they are very vulnerable, poor things, and it says a great deal for a good general that he will make that soil environment as pleasant and homely as possible. Building up the effectiveness of the soil and enhancing the creature comforts of plant roots is the horticultural equivalent of knitting for the armed forces.

Soil is a complex blend of living, once living and never living components and it is with slight diffidence that, in amplifying this statement, I am bound to bring out some of the most unsavoury aspects of modern garden warfare. For those of nervous disposition, may I suggest that you ask an adult to read what follows and interpret it for you in more palatable terms? For I cannot escape discussing an unpleasant truth about the plants whose well-being we strive to serve and whose protection from enemies is the whole *raison d'être* of gardening. They are by nature, I am afraid, all cannibals. Yes, although one may perhaps be able to believe it of an aggressive horse-radish or all-swamping globe thistle, it is difficult to accept that the gentle lettuce or fey lobelia actually lives for preference with its feet in the bodies of the fallen from which it derives much nourishment. And the fallen may be not only the bodies of the enemy, but those of their own compatriots and allies, too.

We have to accept that this is a way of life different from our own; it is not the manner in which we would choose to wage war but I do believe in the importance of accepting others' customs and others' ethics. And if we can manage to look at the matter dispassionately, you will see the innate logic. For if the materials contained in dead plant bodies are not returned to the battleground of the soil, the whole will very soon become grossly impoverished. In the so appropriately named wild world, the bad lands over the garden fence where civilised life must tread warily, such brutish behaviour is everyone's stock in trade, but I am afraid we ignore it at our garden's peril. Civilisation can change things just so far, but plant civilisation has not yet managed to remove the necessity for dead bodies to go back to the soil.

I must now choose my words carefully, for although I have talked of plants actually feeding on the bodies of the fallen, we should realise that this is merely a colloquial way of describing the situation. Despite what plants may think and tell their children, the actual food value of corpses is small and their real benefit derives from the physical effect that they have on the soil itself. It is for this reason that the feeble attempt at imposing our ethic on plants by persuading them to have their remains cremated on bonfires is doomed to failure—such a practice destroys the very physical bulk that is so important. And we are left with a modicum of potash, of use neither to man nor beast, although of very slight benefit to the plants themselves. Digging dead bodies into the soil, however, improves its moisture retentiveness—a benefit equally valuable on a heavy clay and on a light, free-draining sand. And how important this is during the high heat of a

Double digging is of equal benefit on both heavy clay and light, free-draining soils.

summer campaign, when the troops are crying out with thirst and the supply line (or hosepipe) is inadequate. Fighting plants perspire at a quite astonishing rate, and although all carry ration bottles, these are soon exhausted in the sun. With no moist reserves on which to draw, who can blame the infantry if they give up the struggle and quite literally wilt, ultimately to die on their feet? But a moist, cool reserve below makes all the difference and allows the valiant fight to continue unabated.

How can we help our brave troopers? Rather than follow too religiously nature's way and allow dead bodies to rot where they fall, we can at least civilise the operation to the extent of collecting up the corpses at regular intervals, loading them on to the wheelbarrow bier and then allow them the dignity of beginning their decomposition in the graveyard of the **compost bin.** This has a strategic advantage, too, for modern scientific warfare has revealed one particular problem attendant upon allowing freshly dead plants to rot in situ—in starting to rot, they remove nutrient from the soil and so the

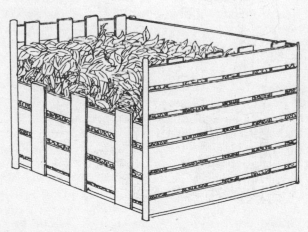

The strategic importance of the compost bin.

very rations that we seek to supplement can in the short term actually be depleted further.

Of course, there are some campaigning gardeners who find their own compost graveyard contains inadequate supplies for the needs of the soil and the plants in their care. There is another ready option available, however. There comes a time in every young gardener's life when he or she must ponder the role of the large black and white cows or brown horses that dine on vegetation beyond the garden boundary (and unfortunately, on rare occasions, within it). What purpose can possibly be served by these slow-moving, armoured objects that consume plant life at an astonishing rate? I have to report that their purpose is solely as mobile, highly automated plant slaughterers for the conversion of slave grasses into corpses faster than you can say Edgar Allan Poe. The mangled organic remains (known colloquially as **manure**) can be purchased from farmers (general dealers in war supplies) who in one of the sadder features of modern life, carry on their disgusting trade quite openly and without any shame. The dead grasses are transported through public streets with only token protest from the populace and will be deposited in steaming heaps close by the battlefield to which they can readily be moved piecemeal. Simple decency suggests that the remains should be given token burial before they are actually put to use, and a few months among the compost works wonders—and as I have mentioned already, this conserves some of the soil food rations, too.

There are those well-meaning commanders who cannot face the thought of handling freshly rotted corpses and who choose to spend their defence budget on pre-packaged soil conditioning—**hop manure**, **mushroom compost**, even **peat**, thinking that these provide a sanitised alternative. But they should be aware that they are fooling themselves. The only difference is that these bags contain corpses longer dead. Hop manure, for instance, is simply the residue of a slave army that was slaughtered once it had fulfilled its allotted short but vigorous campaign. And peat is the compressed mortal remains of armies of even longer ago that died where they fell, fighting in swampy, boggy ground where the anaerobic conditions permitted only the very slightest decay.

In addition to their value in aiding the soil's moisture reserves, compressed corpses have an additional and exceptionally important part to play on the battlefield. For if they are laid thickly over the soil surface, they can actually serve the purpose of smothering occupying weed forces in a highly efficient manner. The value of this technique has been known to campaigning gardeners for centuries but has only recently come to the attention of Shakespearean scholars who long anguished over the meaning of Henry V's call for his troops to 'Close the wall up with our English dead'. Quite clearly this was a ploy to prevent the fortifications of Harfleur from becoming overrun with groundsel.

4   Building Up the Troops

I have already mentioned Napoleon's very accurate observation on military stomachs, and of course the importance of the abdomen in the efficient functioning of mankind is legendary. Remember that when soldiers have finished marching all over their stomachs, their womenfolk turn these same organs to good effect as direct lines of communication to the heart. It should by now be apparent that plants are really no different, the only very slight distinction being that, lacking real stomachs, they use other organs for comparable purposes. But ill-fed plants are feeble beings, as incapable as any other troops of taking on their enemies to optimum effect. So a golden maxim for any garden commander to follow is that, whatever other privations his army must endure, the supply of food rations must not be among them.

Unlike people, plants feed in two main ways and they use, by popular analogy, both their heads and their feet. Their heads are in the air whence they abstract carbon dioxide and water vapour for the production of carbohydrates within their own cells. Their roots and root hairs are in the soil from which come mineral nutrients in aqueous solution. There is a limit to which even a five-star general can affect the composition of the air, although I have encountered regimental sergeant majors whose vocal efforts appeared to represent serious attempts to supplement certain atmospheric gases. But if the actual composition of the air is scarcely alterable, the access to it that individual plant soldiers have is certainly affected by the ways that we manipulate our troops. Nowhere is this better exemplified than on the parade ground of formal bedding. This is a familiar scene in all our great towns and cities and attracts tourists every summer to municipal parks and gardens, where they can admire truly dazzling displays of uniforms. Superficially, the scene is splendid—the thin red line of salvias almost invariably takes the van, usually followed by various South African regiments —pelargonium platoons in dazzling variety and the regal blue of the lobelia detachments, with here and there the bristly armoured uniforms of those ancient European soldiers, the sempervivums. Even humble peasant soldiers like alyssums may sometimes be given a part to play, although they often have to be relieved of their duties before many weeks are past, being unable to match the standards set by their professional companions and revealing their crude origins by actually running to seed in public. Those tourists who get up early enough in the season may be rewarded by one of the most amazing sights in all of horticulture—the changing of the floral guard. This usually takes place in May when the stately ranks of Dutch tulip soldiers that have held the ground over the preceding weeks are unceremoniously dismissed the parade as their once bright uniforms fade in the heat of the spring sunshine.

But I digress; it is too easy to be swayed by the pageantry of it all and forget that within those closeted ranks everything is not what it seems. In the hot, still atmosphere, beneath the weight of heavy uniforms, even the toughest troops can find air hard to come by, and sunlight itself may actually be denied to some of the shorter foreign plants. This is no way to combat an enemy. Time and again, a biological weapon is lobbed by an urban guerilla right into the centre of the parade itself, to open up the ranks in a most destructive way. And remember that the parade ground is only a ceremonial version of war itself—those serried ranks may once have been efficient fighting machines, but in modern battles, slightly greater spaces between the troops will give each a better chance of survival. There is much to be said, too, in a modern garden army, for following the United Nations approach and having mixed soldiery. Troops from different parts of the globe tend to have slightly different food needs (and also tend to be prone to different types of enemy), so a blend of plants of all nations will usually be intrinsically healthier and safer than a monoculture army.

When we turn our attention to ground level, however, and to the minerals that plants derive from beneath their feet, the impact that a gardener can make is immense. And it is here that some of the greatest differences become apparent between civilisation and the uncultured hordes beyond Hadrian's Larch-Lap. For the wild fighting plant is a rough, raw creature, well used to fending for itself, scavenging on the crumbs that fall from passing livestock and adjusted over centuries of hardship to managing on what natural soil can provide. In the civilised world of the garden, we have abandoned such crudeness. Our plants are no longer forced to find their own food and squabble among themselves for the paltry portions of nitrogen, phosphate and potash that they might find in the soil. They have come to expect better and they deserve better, too, for a well-fed plant will always be bigger, stronger, and better able to take care of itself in the hurly-burly of the battlefield. It is unreasonable to expect a good, fit and healthy garden if we don't spend our income wisely and divert a modest portion to military victuals.

It is of course possible for garden leaders and other international estatesmen to go to the opposite extreme and take pains and trouble to ensure that each and every plant has precisely its own specific food requirements. In a few cases, such self-opinionated regiments as the chrysanthemum cavalry have come to expect from their masters not only highly individual meals, but also a regime that necessitates a fresh menu being provided in the mess every few weeks. This is very costly and generally unnecessary, too. **Most plants will thrive happily and rewardingly on a balanced diet** that

Applying a lawn fertiliser with a wheeled spreader.

contains the staples of nitrogen, phosphate and potash. And if helpings are provided twice—once at the start of the annual campaign and once again approximately half-way through, all is usually well. Sometimes additional rations must be rushed to the front in the height of a summer battle when growth is proceeding apace. Then there may not even be time for the troops to eat a normal fertiliser meal served in the usual way on the soil surface, and the nutrients must be supplied partly digested as **liquid fertiliser**. It is important to instruct the regimental cook to adhere strictly to the routine, however, and supply fresh food every season. There is sometimes a temptation to believe that because the plants were well supplied with nutrient last year, they can probably manage with the left-overs in the soil this season, too. Don't be fooled: they can't. For whilst some types of phosphate and potash will certainly lie around for several months, ready and available for passing plants to nibble, nitrogen food certainly will not. Any not eaten promptly will be washed away, almost with the next passing shower.

In this environment- and health-conscious age, it behoves us to think carefully both about the food we eat and the plant food we offer to our charges. There is scarcely a single item of diet that has not at some time been held responsible for one human ailment or other. The relative merits of polyunsaturated fats and cholesterol are now too familiar to bear repetition and, as with most things in life, moderation in cholesterol intake seems to make sense. Almost the horticultural equivalent of cholesterol is nitrogen—excellent in the correct amounts but when taken in excess, prone to encourage soft, feeble tissue, highly prone to biological weapons in particular. So take note, members of the Royal Horticultural Catering Corps, and ensure that all menus are correctly balanced.

Finally, a word about the relative value of so-called **organic** and so-called **artificial fertilisers**. There is a fairly widely held belief that the latter are little better than chemical weapons and will poison the soil and ultimately those who eat the crops. When used extensively, as in civilisations founded on slavery (commercial farming, for instance), there may well be some truth in this. But in civilised gardens, moderate use of manufactured or even junk (compound) fertilisers is permissible. It should not be forgotten that our plant troops have a relatively undiscerning palate and cannot in fact tell the source of their nitrogen, phosphate and potash. It is rather like being able to taste eggs but not to be able to distinguish between an omelette and a lemon meringue.

5   *Structural Defences*

There must be many instances in the history of warfare when the simplest solution to a problem has proved the most effective, even if it has been the last for anyone to try. I have already expressed my distaste for chemical warfare, even for chemical defence, and I am constantly saddened when gardeners choose it as the first option, almost irrespective of the nature of the enemy. There are several instances when a physical obstruction is cheaper, environmentally much more acceptable and in the final analysis more effective. Think of tank traps for a start . . .

Clearly, the physical approach to garden defence will vary enormously depending on the type and source of the attack. A two-metre fence will not keep out a squadron of bullfinches any more than wire netting will deter slugs. It is a matter of courses for horses. And mention of horses prompts me to start with the really big barriers, ranging from Hadrian's Larch-Lap to the Great Wall of Suburbia or even, on a rambling country estate, Offa's Ha-Ha itself. Curiously enough, the larger the barrier, the less effective it seems to be at keeping out small pests which are attracted to small nooks and crannies like moths to a lamp (of which more shortly). A wide open boundary may be ignored totally by wandering woodlice or marauding maggots, but once a barrier is erected, this is clearly detectable on aerial photographs and so draws attention to itself with the result that the enemy sends forth special detachments specifically to find a way through. What, then, will a big barrier exclude? If it is two metres high it will keep out most of the terrestrial mammalian tank regiments such as rabbits, dogs or even deer. It will be useless against cats unless the subtle ploy is adopted of stretching a single strand of wire about five centimetres above the top rail. This gives the ferocious feline nowhere to balance and its attacks are repulsed in a trice. For the most effective exclusion of the rabbit menace, however, wire netting is needed, buried to a depth of about 30 centimetres to prevent them from tunnelling beneath. Unfortunately, burial is no deterrent to the mole, the sinister black peril of modern warfare, for he can tunnel to very considerable depths and undermine the most carefully constructed barriers.

There are some garden plants that are so vulnerable to attack that they seem almost to have a death wish. Raspberries, blackcurrants and other soft fruit are quite simply so stupid as to be their own worst enemies, and I am afraid that they really must be locked up for their own good. Stone walls may not their prison make but plastic netting will certainly suffice for their cage. In fact, despite my aversion to plastic warfare in general, the **fruit cage** is one instance where the light weight of plastic is a very real benefit, but it really does need to be kept closed throughout the season's campaign. Bullfinches and their allies will launch attacks at fruit buds, open flowers, ripening fruit and even young leaves on occasion, so there really is almost no period when the proverbial chains can be loosened. I sometimes see perfunctory efforts made by beleaguered gardeners at protecting blackcurrants and other fruit bushes merely by throwing netting over them, but this just underestimates the enemy's ability to find a way through. A cage really is the only answer, although that other ridiculous liability, the strawberry, can manage with net-covered cloche-style protectors. The **cloche** itself provides protection of a sort, but it is scarcely an impenetrable barrier and once an enemy has found its way inside, it too benefits from the protection and may even be encouraged to set up home and multiply.

Small invaders can sometimes be combated very effectively with small barriers—the one-footed slug can actually be

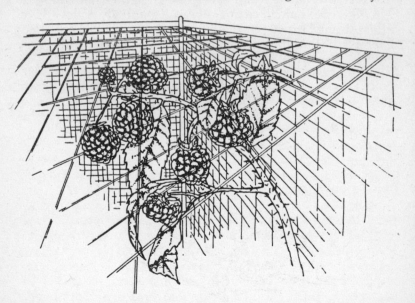

The fruit cage is one instance where the light weight of plastic is a very real benefit.

wrong-footed simply by placing finely prickled twigs or powdery ash or soot in its way. And that wholly untrustworthy aerial attacker, the earwig, can be lured into hay or straw jammed into small upturned plant pots placed on bamboo canes amongst dozing dahlias. I sometimes despair both with dahlias and with chrysanthemums. They have become so obsessed with the finery of their own uniforms that they forget that those deep, curled petals present a temptation no passing earwig can resist.

Perhaps the most interesting of all garden defensive barriers is that based on the barrage balloon principle. Carefully collated results from years of intelligence gathering have revealed hitherto only half-suspected facts about the performance of enemy aircraft. It has, for instance, been discovered that the deadly all-weather fighter known by its NATO code name, carrot fly, is essentially a low level attacker only. If a 60 centimetre high fence of polythene sheet is erected around a settlement of carrots, they can be very

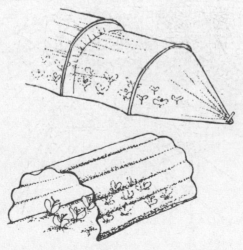

The cloche provides protection of a sort, but it is not an impenetrable barrier.

effectively protected and suffer only the disturbance of hearing carrot flies crashing into the screen all day long.

There are two other physical approaches to the repulsion of enemy forces once the barrier has proved ineffective. The first is what in modern gardening warfare is termed a repellent but in years gone by, when men were men and not afraid to call a spade a spade, it was much more freely admitted that the principle was that of frightening the foe to death. The procedures are seen less often in gardens nowadays than on the serious campaign ground of the allotment—for after all, it is only the really serious battles that are fought in someone else's territory. Simplest of the enemy frighteners is a device that owes much to the ancient

The deep, curled petals of the chrysanthemum are a temptation no passing earwig can resist.

pagan origins of gardening: an effigy intended to make the gardener appear even larger and more horrible than he really is. Unfortunately its name, the scarecrow, has become an anomaly, for the crow is an enemy of the past and even its modern equivalents, the pigeon, blue tit, starling and bullfinch, never actually admit to finding the thing particularly scaring. More frequently to be seen nowadays are various crude products of the Home Guard, in particular the waving of blue plastic flags from bamboo cane poles, an operation as unsightly as it is useless. I do believe in a neat and tidy garden battlefield and cannot find myself in sympathy with these bizarre attempts to produce horticultural reconstructions of the US marines capturing Iwo Jima.

But the second physical approach to garden defence is a more drastic resort for it can result only in the death of the invaders. **Traps** come in various shapes and sizes and use many different devices to lure the enemy to his fate. The mole trap is probably the crudest but it is certainly effective when used by a professional anti-terrorist soldier or mole catcher. The mouse trap provides an almost infallible method of eliminating not only mice but voles too. But it is a weapon to be used cautiously, for it has an unpleasant habit of exploding in the hands of the person placing it. The mouse and the vole are among the most innately cunning of garden enemies and they will not blunder blindly into traps. Despite the ancient military tradition of placing cheese in the trap, the best lure is usually bread.

Perhaps the most effective yet most underused of garden battle traps is the **slug trap**, a small item of hardware that plays on the age-honoured fondness of troops everywhere for alcoholic beverage. The principle has been used since time immemorial to lure soldiers into trouble, and the present-day gardening version comprises a series of small jars filled with beer and sunk to their rims among a platoon of lettuces. This will trap dozens of nocturnal raiding parties of mollusc commandoes.

Finally to two very special procedures concerned with the luring of flying invaders. Whilst employing searchlights to scan the night sky for passing aphids might be a fruitless exercise, light holds a magnetic charm for insects of many kinds, and in some parts of the world small lamp traps are used among crops to lure pests. The technique is used little in British gardens and this may be because of the great destruction that can be wrought on beneficial insect troops from our own side. But from the hotbeds of military thinking has come an appliance so devious and debasing in its technology that I have had to think very hard indeed about the correctness of introducing it into a military gardening manual that may fall into the hands of minors. I have in mind the Mata Hari trap, a device that lures unsuspecting insects to their fate by the promise of sexual favours, suggested by baiting it with sex hormones. How much lower can modern garden warfare stoop?

6 The Good Companions— An Entertainment

Every worthwhile campaign must have its lighter moments. It is important that the troops should be entertained by visiting performers and gardening is no different; it needs its ENSA, too. On the face of it, their task is particularly difficult; it isn't easy to laugh while horsetail is overwhelming your leeks, or smile as your dahlias disappear under a party of foraging earwigs. But we are a stoic race, quite at home with the brave face and cheerfulness in adversity. Over the years, I have seen many attempts made at causing amusement to embattled gardeners. I can recall the bonsai sunflower of a few years back and some pretty astonishing weapons, including the long-handled, spring-loaded Australian daisy grubber and the leaky hose-pipe manufactured from re-cycled Icelandic car tyres. I suppose the influx of about fifty new African and French marigold varieties every year would entertain some, although I find it merely depressing. But lawnmower advertisements are certainly always good for a chuckle—it is the painted lawn stripes that do it. And the illustrations on seed packets are either disgusting or funny, depending on your sense of humour.

But if there is one reliable standby to bring a grin to the face of a gardening Tommy, it must be companion planting. I could take all day recounting companionship stories but must limit myself to a few of the real classics. The underlying theme of all of these stories is the same—that you can defeat the enemy or at least keep him at bay by using certain carefully orchestrated combinations of troops. As with all the best funny stories, there was originally a grain of truth in the notion, but it has become distorted beyond recognition until there are now some (especially those involving garlic) that can be guaranteed to bring tears to your eyes.

To be fair, perhaps I should mention the biggest grain of truth first. There is a species of South American *Tagetes* called *T. minuta*—a pretty small thing as you may guess (and indeed, a small pretty thing too). This is an interesting plant and it has the ability to produce a substance with some anti-eelworm effect. Not against all eelworms may it be said, and not against other types of enemy troop either, but a slight effect nonetheless. Because of this interesting attribute, however, the story has grown up that tagetes in general will control pretty well any sort of pest you care to name. The reputation has even spread to the whole of the wretched marigold tribe and, thinking again of those dozens of new varieties launched by seed companies every year, I can even think of a possible source of the rumour. No, perish the thought.

But this companionship business now goes very much further. Have you heard the one about the nasturtiums and the whiteflies? The story goes something along the lines

Tagetes minuta, *responsible for the myth that all marigolds will control any pest you care to name.*

of—if you plant nasturtiums with tomatoes (or even other plants, too), then by some magic means, whiteflies will be frightened away. I knew a poor gardener who tried this once. Every year the tomatoes in his greenhouse were laid low by the little white terrors and every counter-measure he tried had failed. Until one day he heard about the nasturtium effect. As it happened, he had some climbing nasturtium seeds left over, so he sowed these around his ring culture pots. The tomatoes, understandably, didn't comment, but the whiteflies took a liking to the nasturtiums and began to multiply on them even faster than they had done on the tomatoes. Then the nasturtiums decided that the warm, cosy greenhouse made a pleasant change from the great outdoors, and it obviously reminded them of what they do to tomatoes in their common ancestral home in South America: they strangled them.

Now try this one for size—garlic will eradicate peach leaf curl. If only this could be true, for peach leaf curl is one of the most effective and depressing biological weapons in the whole of garden warfare. But you too can banish it if you plant garlic beneath your peach and almond trees. Before you actually split your sides, I should say that there have been a few occasions when I have known garlic to flourish particularly well and peach leaf curl to be less than serious. But I should also say that this has invariably been during hot, dry summers when the peach leaf curl weapon has a tendency to misfire and when garlic tends to grow rather well. And can you imagine the concentration of chemical emissions that would be needed to drift upwards from the garlic plants to inactivate the leaf curl fungus? Concentrated French dressing wouldn't be in the same league. There must be something especially amusing about garlic (although it eludes me), for it is also claimed to keep roses free from aphid attack. Here the explanation really is a show stopper—the roots of the roses absorb the garlic emission from the soil and their sap thus becomes unattractive to the aphids. And whilst you pick yourself up, I should add that the handbook of garden battlefield tactics from which I am quoting, adds the rider that this can be done without any fear that the perfume of the roses themselves will be affected.

Garlic will also lure the black peril, or mole, from his burrows, according to many ancient garden warfare references; but then so will old kippers, orange peel, moth balls and numerous other types of strongly smelling ammunition. Perhaps the best one about moles concerns the caper spurge, for there is a strong rumour that if you import a squad of these rather stark, upright troops, no mole will dare to pass under your frontier. The truth was finally revealed by an excellent horticultural general of my acquaintance, who was on a scouting party in a neighbour's territory when he saw a caper spurge move as if of its own volition. Within a few minutes, the culprit was revealed as none other than a mole, who was in the process of raising his periscope immediately beneath the aforesaid repellent.

One of the most ingenious yet widespread of the many peasant controls for anti-brassica mines (clubroot) is a real chuckle. Place a stick of rhubarb in the dibble hole when planting your cabbages and the mines are inactivated; so says the tale. Many years ago, I decided to try this and so, in full disguise (so as not to alarm my troops into thinking their commanding officer had finally swapped his brains for compost), popped carefully measured lengths of *Rheum cultorum* into the company of my brassica roots. I thought carefully through the reasoning: anti-brassica mines are most easily activated by an acidic soil; but rhubarb itself is acidic, so is some localised explosion to be expected? Does the rhubarb itself become affected with clubroot? Or is the effect due to a strong concentration of some other astringent substance in the leaves? I could scarcely wait while the experimental weapon ran its seasonal course. After two months, I uprooted the cabbages; the suspense was killing. Something had certainly exploded the mines but the result was the largest clubroot symptoms I had ever seen. I didn't even bother with the hospital and sent the whole sad battalion straight to the mortuary.

Whilst on the subject of the brassica brigade, allow me just one final fling before closing time. What did the turnip do to the couch grass? Answer: it controlled it; yes, controlled it. There's one to tell to your grandchildren—over an area of garden occupied with couch, make a thick sowing of turnip seed. I once tried that one, too—and ended up with an even denser mass of couch grass and enough turnips to keep old man Townshend happy for weeks.

But that's enough light entertainment for one war; back to the serious business again. Although, although—there is one final adage that I might just mention in passing. Did someone once say something about the truth of words spoken in jest? Surely he couldn't have been a gardener, could he?

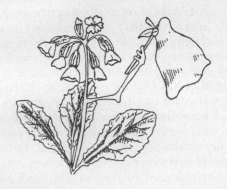

7   Controlled Surrender

It is said that only the British can make glory out of defeats. And over the years such events as the Charge of the Light Brigade and Dunkirk seem to prove the notion correct. But surrender is something rather different, and any military man would much rather dress this up in more appealing terms—by calling it temporary, strategic or controlled, for instance. In one aspect of garden warfare, such a controlled surrender has become a fact of life for many gardeners in recent seasons. In fact there are gardens in which the surrender has been so sudden, so willingly entered into and so complete that I am not sure that it isn't really some very subtle form of pre-emptive strike.

I would be the last to advocate surrender in the face of some of the enemies we have to confront, although when in due course I come to consider the wording of peace treaties and truces, there will inevitably have to be some giving of ground. I cannot at present conceive of making concessions to slugs or millepedes, or accepting that cats and deer can have free access to my territory. But I shall reserve final judgement on that for the moment. It is the occupying weed forces that concern me here and the quite extraordinary effect that enemy propaganda has had on gardening attitudes to them over the past ten years or so. Those who, within very recent history, would have been branded fifth columnists, or even called traitors, now seem to be considered perfectly respectable members of horticultural society. I cannot fight this trend forever so I must recognise its strategic importance.

In essence, the changed situation is that, whilst every wild plant was once considered an occupying enemy, there are now gardeners who either tolerate them or, in many cases, actually clasp the wild vegetation to their bosoms. I have to admit, although the words stick in the gullet, that there are even some gardens where total surrender has taken place and civilisation really has vanished as the wild world has been allowed or encouraged to retake the territory. I cannot reconcile gardening with the latter state of affairs: it is the total negation of all that centuries of advanced botanical thinking and philosophy have come to represent. And yet an expression has even been devised to describe such a land, a domain under the jackboot of tyranny, crushed beneath the heels of shepherd's purse, thistle and dock. It is laughably called a **wild garden**, a term directly analogous to and about as meaningful as a slave democracy. The correct expression for such a post-cataclysmic world is wilderness. Owners (I cannot bring myself to call them gardeners) of such places are shameless individuals who do not even hide away their woeful neglect by confining it to the back of the plot (I can no longer call it a garden), but brazenly display their spineless capitulation to passers-by at the front as well. What examples to set to the cadet gardeners of the next generation. Small

109

wonder that hooligans and vandals commit murder daily in our streets, decapitating trees, uprooting innocent wallflowers and even mugging lettuces and carrots unprotected on the fringes of allotments.

But whilst I shrink from sitting around the negotiating table with such miscreants, I would be failing in my responsibility if I didn't talk face to face with those who feel that, whilst a garden is still a garden, there may be some room in it for peasant troops. I have to say, nonetheless, that these peasants will be always be an unruly bunch, in constant need of attention and never really to be trusted. Their manners will be rough, their morals suspect. Witness the hordes of self-sown, undisciplined infants always to be seen around their feet, as likely as not even to invade your hallowed turf.

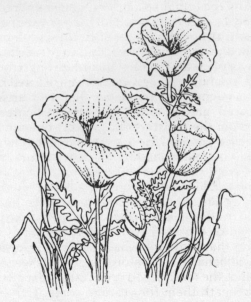

There may be room in the garden for a few peasant troops, such as the field poppy, but they can never really be trusted.

One thing must be made perfectly clear, however. Whilst you may be disposed to give over part of your garden to peasant civilians, be warned very strongly against allowing access to their professional weed soldiery. Among civilians I include such creatures as wild geraniums, meadowsweet, heartsease and cowslip, which are usually simple but fairly peaceful individuals, only occasionally taking up arms in an irregular, vigilante capacity.

What concerns me greatly is the listings of soldiers and weapons to be found in the catalogues of international arms dealers or seed companies. I have already condemned some of the illustrations in these publications as little better than low grade pornography. The impact of seeing for the first time what the caption described as a 'champion pumpkin' is with me still. And the tomato plant with a one hundred-fruit truss must surely have been retouched. I can only hope that no one will be foolish enough to leave such things lying around the potting shed where young seedlings might see them. But my present worry is that professional fighting troops such as bindweed, celandine and ground elder are listed for sale, too. Can you imagine the problems that will arise when an inexperienced garden officer, a junior lieutenant newly emerged from the register office, takes command of his first semi-detached posting? He is swayed by the flowery descriptions, anxious to demonstrate his horticultural manhood to his new young wife who wills him on to play his part in conserving wildlife and making for a better world. He fills in his order, sends off the draft and receives his purchases, ominously under plain brown wrapper. The troops are liberated into the prepared barrack-ground in the full expectation that they will behave as his military manuals say soldiers will behave. But before he can say 'weedkiller', they are off and the entire territory falls beneath them; and remains beneath them for years to come.

I am bound to say that the handling of peasants is something to be undertaken only by the more experienced

Stinging nettles are a lure for butterflies, but keep them strictly controlled.

among gardening top brass, but there are certain rules of command that I feel I should give. There is much to be said for placing the better-looking peasants amongst civilised communities, where their roughness will be dulled in the overall impact. Alternatively, it is possible to group together several different peasants in the same compound, because this facilitates the imposition of the rather unusual discipline and management that they require. For whilst a civilised army performs better on a normal healthy diet of nitrogen, phosphate and potash, peasants are unused to such fare and will suffer severely if it is given to them. They are, for instance, quite likely to throw off their parade ground uniforms and wear nothing but leafy battle dress. And in consequence, they can actually provide almost sitting targets for biological weapons fired over the nearest frontier. Peasants are accustomed to deriving all their bodily requirements from unamended soil, so do remember **never to serve them fertiliser**; it may seem cruel to those brought up in a different environment, but it really is for their own good.

There is one particularly difficult and contentious area, however, into which some are willing to admit peasants, even peasant soldiers, but where to my mind they are playing with fire. For the very nerve centre of any garden, its lawn, is sometimes given over to these crude troops, for no other reason than that the green uniform of its proper inhabitants is considered boring. I find it hard to choose words appropriate to such sacrilege. The very thought of seeing yellow and white jackets dotted among the smooth green velvet uniforms worn by the elite lawn regiments of fescue is almost more than a hardened garden militarist can swallow. I must reiterate the basically untrustworthy nature of these outsiders. Give them a centimetre and they will claim a hectare. Once you have offered them board and bedding in your lawn, you will sooner or later be faced with civil disturbance on a

I find it hard to choose appropriate words to describe the sacrilege of allowing dandelions and daisies to encroach onto your hallowed turf.

grand scale and, be assured, the time will come when you have to resort to using chemical defence to try and make good the harm they have wrought. Use peasants in your garden if you will, but be warned of the consequences if you turn your back for more than a season.

8　The Resistance Movement

There is more than one way to kill a cat and a change is as good as a rest. Two metaphors for one chapter are quite adequate, so I shall now amplify both with a truism—there is more than one way to defeat an enemy. So far, I have concentrated largely on methods based in some way on direct confrontation with your foes. You can erect barriers to keep them out, install traps to trap them or actually obliterate them by using chemical artillery. But there is another approach, a procedure innately more cunning and clever but one that depends for its successful deployment on a fairly high level of sophisticated military intelligence and in some instances necessitates some rather major activity on the part of the Royal Garden Engineers. For convenience, I shall group together all such approaches under the umbrella heading of resistance, although it is resistance that takes various rather distinct forms.

First, there is the problem that I discussed at some length earlier, the natural hazards that beset any army sooner or later. The **climate**, the **soil**, the **terrain**, the **aspect** of the garden, are all features that can militate against the successful use of certain particular types of plant. Let's examine the soil in particular.

Of course, the various operations that I discussed under trench warfare will make life easier for the troops deployed in any particular place, but there will always be some battalions that you just cannot use in certain regions. For over the centuries of international horticultural conflict, some of the most sophisticated and glamorous of all troops have come to require very special conditions in which to operate. Given these conditions, many of them can cope with a very high proportion of the weapons thrown against them. Denied these conditions, they will be miserable, pathetic objects of neither use nor ornament. The greatest dilemma and frustration attends the gardener with a naturally chalky site. Understandably, he wants the finest soldiers that money can buy and when he has travelled to foreign parts and seen acid gardens, the hankering becomes almost unbearable. But time after time, despite extensive government publicity, grave mistakes (I use the term advisedly) are made. On a visit to a troop recruitment office or garden centre, the most splendid rhododendrons, kalmias, pieris, azaleas and camellias are found to be freely available, often for a very modest signing on fee. Even lesser soldiery, such as summer-flowering heathers, look as if they are positively begging to be taken away. The garden commander himself has no resistance to such pleadings, so he signs the contract and transports them home. Quickly he double-checks his rules of engagement and finds they are unambiguous. These troops must have acid conditions, so what can be done now?

It is at this stage that a telegram must be sent quickly to the

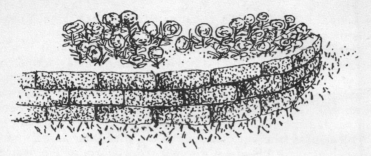

A peat bed, the Bailey bridge of modern gardening.

engineers. They will arrive, post haste, with the necessary hardware—spade, fork, a pile of logs and several bales of peat—ready for the swift erection of the Bailey bridge of modern gardening, a **peat bed**. This provides the opportunity to give the elite new troops a worthy home, for the logs are used to confine a small area of garden bed. Within this, the peat is dug thoroughly into the underlying soil and, provided a little special ration is given early each season in the form of sequestered iron, the newcomers will flourish. I would ask only that the commanding officer, seeing his fine new detachment, doesn't become over-enthusiastic and expect to import *Rhododendron sino-grande* or its kind, fully 12 metres tall.

The gardener with an acid soil has much less of a problem if he wishes to adapt the environment to enable him to use some of the chalk loving species like clematis. First, this is because they are much less demanding in their requirements and will tolerate acidity much better than acid lovers will tolerate lime. But second, because it is relatively easy to increase the alkalinity of an acid battlefield by using the scorched earth policy of **spreading lime**.

Relatively few types of soldiery take readily to fighting in a wet environment. There should of course, in every wet garden, be a small unit of marine commandoes such as lysichitons and callas that revel in doing battle in such conditions. But the remainder of the garden army will

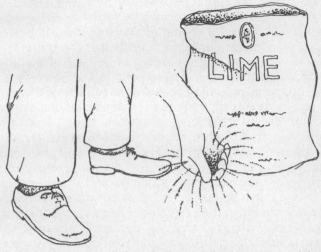

It is relatively easy to increase alkalinity by the scorched earth policy of spreading lime.

inevitably be placed at a singular disadvantage if their boots become waterlogged. This will slow down their advance, render them less amenable to feeding properly and leave them otherwise ill-equipped to defend themselves against almost any type of invading force. The answer lies in yet another task for the Garden Engineers, although one that is undertaken rather less frequently than I would expect. Installing a **garden drainage system** is no longer the major military operation that once it was. Many a gardener has blenched at the prospect of having his territory wholly dug up; especially when the excavation must inevitably be extended to include the holy of holies, the lawn. Times have changed and modern military factories have yielded up the almost instant drainage system, the answer to many a battlefield commander's prayer.

But I must now turn my attention to a deeper subject, and pay tribute to the research laboratories of official military establishments, which have looked for novel ways to defeat the enemy. If you find it hard to stop him, find it hard or even distasteful to kill him, there are two further options open to you. One is to find a means of avoiding him altogether and launch your major periods of horticultural activity at a time when the foe is resting or waging a campaign elsewhere. The second is to develop weapon-resisting armour that he is unable to penetrate. In order to make full use of the potential offered by the former, it is essential to undertake careful study of the information contained in books describing the modus operandi of your enemy (guide books to garden pests and diseases, for instance). From these you will learn, for example, that the most intense slug warfare campaigns rarely begin before the end of the summer, and that to protect the otherwise more or less defenceless potato, you may have to restrict yourself to the early varieties and leave the maincrop to gardens with dry, slug-less terrain. I always think the potato is something of a garden warfare liability anyway. It is very much a creature of the summer, but even then its perpetually somnolent attitude reveals the *mañana* philosophy of its South American homeland. To be perfectly honest, I would not be averse to denying it real battleground room altogether and raising a few very early varieties imprisoned in large tubs.

There are relatively few examples of plants having developed armour that effectively resists the depredations of chewing enemies, although rather more have some value against sucking pests. Some raspberry varieties, for instance, diminish slightly their gardening liability by being resistant to the attacks of aphids and, of course, thus avoiding the germ warfare weapons that they carry. But resistance to biological weapons is rather more widespread and is in many instances now taken for granted. If you look carefully at nineteenth century manuals of gardening military conduct, you will find frequent reference to snapdragons succumbing to the attacks of rust, whereas the modern fighting snapdragon is rarely affected. Mildew attacks on Michaelmas daisies need not be a

The modern snapdragon is rarely affected by rust.

serious problem either, now that varieties are available well able to turn away the mildew missiles. But always scrutinise military hardware manuals carefully before committing yourself to purchases—not all agents describe their wares very carefully and it is sensible to purchase from a reputable supplier who actually explains the military strengths and weaknesses of the various troops on offer.

9   Superiority of Numbers

When I was at school, there was a popular story about two
rabbits being pursued by a pack of hounds. As the two
bunnies paused for breath behind a tree stump, one said to
the other, 'Well, what do we do—keep going and try to outrun
them, or stay here and try to outnumber them?' Undoubtedly,
sheer force of numbers has been a valuable attribute in many
battles over the centuries, and if the numerical odds are
tipped very heavily in your enemy's favour, his army usually
becomes a 'horde'; quite possibly a pagan or infidel horde. But
this sort of advantage can work both ways. Suppose the
invaders entering your garden are present in such quantities
that it really does prove quite impossible to keep them in
check with conventional weapons; or suppose that for well-
founded ethical or even religious reasons, you are opposed to

chemical defence. Should you not bring to mind another old tale, this time a gardening adage of some substance, although one that few gardeners will realise has an origin in military strategy? 'One for the rook, one for the crow, one to die and one to grow' is one version; 'One to rot and one to grow, one for pigeon and one for crow' is another. The message of both is loud and clear.

I suppose the philosophy is in some ways comparable with that of allowing the opposition slight territorial gains to lull them into a false sense of security before striking back with renewed vengeance. On the other hand, I suppose the less charitable could see it as a sort of limited surrender; of sacrificing a few of the troops so that civilisation as a whole can survive. Donate some of your apples to the codling moth in return for a few wholesome fruit, perhaps. I am proposing to take an even more charitable overview of the whole policy. No garden commander can, in the final analysis, adopt a genuine attitude towards the opposition of 'live and let live',

Donate some of your apples to the codling moth in return for a few wholesome fruit, if you're lucky.

for his garden would thus cease to exist and the very reason for living would vanish beneath those alien hordes. We cannot stop the enemies at our gate and over our fence from pursuing their policy towards our plant population. It is in their nature and part of their *raison d'être* that they should invade our gardens. Of course, if we do nothing at all, we shall be masters of nought, or at best of a wilderness. But why should we necessarily respond in like fashion? Why should we lower ourselves to the level of the other side? Surely, if we raise our moral stance we can actually allow other species to survive whilst still maintaining horticultural civilisation. There are two ways to tackle this. One is the purely **numerical approach** that concerns me here. The second is in actually suing for peace and negotiating a **truce** at the very least; this I shall consider in the final chapter.

In the straightforward numbers game, there is a difficult balance to be struck. Just how many extra beans, lettuces, cabbages do you require to satisfy the enemy and yet ensure that the indigenous populace doesn't go hungry? Will the foreign army not work to parkinsonian precepts and send in more troops (or multiply the existing ones) until the whole of your squadrons are eliminated? Are you not providing them with nothing more than a foothold or bridgehead from which they can strike further? You may well be; it is a dangerous game to play and on balance I would have to say that the old adage is probably not far from right—you may well need to sacrifice every three rows in order to harvest one. I am not sure that I find this particularly appealing; it requires the approach of the man who always backs the one to three odds-on chance and yet still loses from time to time.

Perhaps there are other ways. One option is to provide alternative decoy targets, rather in the manner of dummy rocket launching sites or false maps conveniently lost in enemy territory; in fact to turn to your advantage the principle of disinformation that I have discussed already as a common enemy tactic. But this is not particularly easy either.

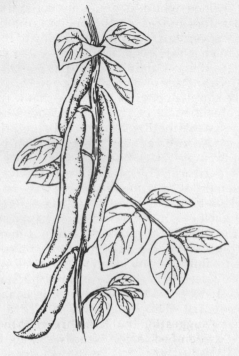

How many extra broad beans do you require to satisfy the enemy?

For reasons that have long puzzled me, there is something intrinsically attractive to enemy soldiers about garden plants that nothing else seems able to replace. For instance, in the wild world beyond the Great Wall of Suburbia, that so innocent-looking enemy flying machine, the large white butterfly, is more than content to direct its attacks against almost all types of plant in the family Cruciferae. Yet you can plant charlock, hedge mustard and any other related peasant species you care to name all over your garden, and the wretched aerial menaces will still always seek out your brassica patch. Why is it that their non-military counterpart, the green-veined white, is generally content to stay with peasant crucifers and leave your civilians unharmed? I don't know the answer, but it means that trying to fool the enemy in this manner is rarely successful.

So perhaps there is another ploy that we can try. Suppose we adopt as a matter of principle the essential role of direct counter-measures; suppose we concede that we must remove, eradicate or kill some of the enemy troops by physical or chemical defensive methods; but that we limit this action in a deliberate and concerted way. Perhaps I can best illustrate this by an example taken from a real battle of which I have personal experience. The garden territory in question had a high population of cauliflowers. Now I have to concede that the cauliflower is something of a prima donna. It always considers itself a cut above its brassica relatives, looking down on the cabbage in a very supercilious manner, looking up to the Brussels sprout only in a purely physical sense and never even admitting any relationship at all with the slave hordes of oil-seed rape that constantly hammer at garden gates and fences in a most uncultured fashion, as if demanding entry. The cauliflower is also a fickle thing, resenting any suggestion that it might care to move from cold frame into garden bed (often actually sulking for weeks on end when forced to do so), and positively demanding that its thirst be slaked constantly. The garden in question had suffered every summer since time immemorial from wave after wave of assaults by large whites (butterflies, not pigs). But the garden commander was a lady of high principles, no bloodthirsty amazon who could adopt a scorched earth approach. She had a moral sense of responsibility to global animal-kind and so she planted two rows of cabbages next to her cauliflowers. (She didn't like cabbages, as it happened, but that is not material to the tactic.)

As the predictable early season invasions came and the caterpillar raiding parties made their first appearance, the lady commander counter-attacked. She left the cabbages alone; this didn't actually divert any attack from the smug-looking cauliflowers but it salved her conscience. First she used a straightforward physical response against the caterpillars with two of the most ingenious weapons ever devised, the finger and thumb. But after a week or so, this pest collection system was clearly not working—there were always more of them hidden away beneath the folds of leaves. So the C-in-C brought out the anti-riot squad with their water-cannon and attempted to blast the caterpillars away. This had several effects. All the caterpillars ended up much cleaner than they had started, some drowned, some displayed a Bonnington-like ability to climb back up again, the lady commander became extremely wet; and the cauliflowers still looked smug. Eventually she was forced to employ chemical defence, and as this event took place a few years ago, the least noxious chemical weapon she could find was derris, a natural plant product, of course. (Not that this is necessarily a good advertisement; after all, strychnine and heroin are plant products, too). Today, seeking an environmentally respectable caterpillar slayer, she might have used a biological defensive weapon—a spray containing a bacterial culture. But the moral of the story is clear; you can keep a clear conscience by making a gesture towards conserving your enemy but you can't win the war solely by trying to outnumber him.

10 The Truce

Every good war must come to an end sometime. I realise that there are many occasions when the day-to-day struggle might seem merely a drop in a hundred years of mixed metaphors, but even the real Hundred Years' War had its off-moments. I don't know if the English and the French actually had intermediate peace treaties, but in gardening there is much to be said for calling a halt every now and then. Before you board the plane for Geneva, however, it is important to understand your own position. First, you must have the full agreement of your own Parliament; there is nothing worse than a gardening household divided against itself, or of an understanding reached in the Lower House (potting shed) being vetoed by the Upper Chamber (kitchen). You must decide quite clearly if you are going to sue for peace on any

127

terms (unconditional surrender), if there is to be give and take
on both sides, or if you are simply seeking a temporary truce.
The problem with a truce comes with enforcement and
validity of motive—if there have been few attacks of aphids
recently, does this mean that you are actually winning the
struggle or merely that the weather has been against aerial
warfare generally? And can you in all honesty say that you do
want peace and not just a breathing space whilst new supplies
of derris are delivered to the garden centre?

Once at the negotiating table, once the talks about talks
about talks have been concluded and the real business begins,
how much are you prepared to concede? This will depend, of
course, on the nature of the war itself and of the weapons
that have been deployed against you. I must confess that I
would find it hard to sit down and talk about peace while

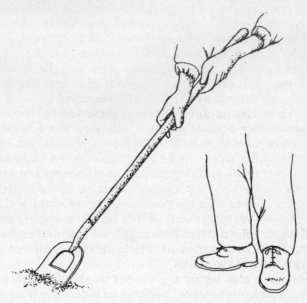

You could agree to rely on conventional weed control measures such as the hoe.

there was still a significant occupying weed force on my land. I might be prepared to allow a few lightweight annual troops as part of a continuing low-level enemy presence, but to seek a settlement on the basis of a well-entrenched population of bindweed would be political as well as military folly. How could you hold up your head again in the great international debating chamber of the village horticultural society? And how could you again seek a mandate from the electorate to serve on the allotment committee, knowing that you still had couch in your cabbages? Even if you sign a treaty to the effect that you will renounce the routine use of chemical anti-weed defences and rely on conventional measures such as the hoe, there must be provision for you to keep a small weedkiller reserve in case of insurgent terrorist activity.

The possession of at least one chemical anti-weed missile is especially critical if the integrity of the heart of all civilisation is to remain inviolate. No treaty can possibly be allowed to impose an obligation for you to have daisies on your lawn, for that is the stuff of nightmares and ghoulish gardening. I must confess my continued astonishment at the fact that books and other literature containing full-colour photographs of such disgusting situations are still freely displayed.

And I think the option must remain for you to employ one chemical defence against aerial attack, even if you undertake not to use it as a first resort. **Derris** or **pyrethrum** are the substances most likely to be acceptable to the opposition's negotiators. I think you can concede a willingness not to cross your frontier to make a pre-emptive strike against nettles or similar units, even if do they exercise uncomfortably close to home. But conversely, there should be a firm understanding that all dandelions must maintain at least 100 metres distance from national boundaries to minimise the impact of spontaneous parachute assaults.

There must also be an agreement to allow you one anti-biological defensive weapon; perhaps an olden-day instrument like **Bordeaux Mixture** which served the French so well in the

Great Grape War of blessed memory. I think that any treaty must also concede an exception in the case of the defence of the Royal Family, the house of Rose. They really should be protected at all costs, for centuries of inbreeding have left them so very vulnerable to the unpleasant things of life. A weapon that provides them with protection both from biological mildew and air-borne aphid attack would be ideal.

So much for the demands you must make of the enemy and the points you might be prepared to concede. What positive gestures can you offer in order to persuade him to turn his wrath aside to the next door neighbour's garden? I think it would be reasonable for you to promise not to grow plants

Concentrate on plants like daffodils that will naturalise.

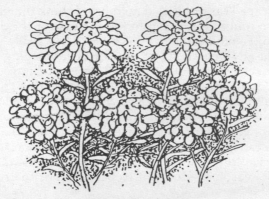

Plump for flowers like candyftuft that will self-seed forever.

that struggle to find a home in your garden and to concentrate on those like daffodils that will naturalise, or like candytuft that will self-seed forever. You may just have to dismantle your peat bed and grow instead the winter flowering heathers, and also undertake not to apply any lime for at least five years. Such gestures could carry some weight, especially if the enemy is rather dependent on propaganda to further his struggle. But against a really heavily armed foe, rather more serious decisions will have to made. It might just be that if there are airfields of commercial rape or cabbage crops nearby, the threat from the squadrons of large whites will always be overwhelming. Difficult as it would be, you could offer to give up the growing of brassicas. Similarly, continued all-weather attacks by carrot flies might mean you actually having to put your carrots onto the negotiating table. If, by grave misfortune, biological mines have been sown in your vegetable plot, I am afraid that even the most contrite of enemies will be unable to defuse them. This will therefore certainly spell the end of either brassicas or onions, depending on the type of mine used—the clubroot or white-rot mine respectively being primed to act specifically against these two important types of plant.

Abandon your peat bed and grow the lime-tolerant winter flowering heather instead of its acid-loving, summer flowering colleague.

Then there is the major problem of undisciplined enemy soldiery. I have yet to meet a commanding officer who is really in control of his slugs. They are so unpredictable in their habits and of course are nocturnal, a feature that presents special problems to those less well endowed armies with no provision for night vision binoculars among the officers' equipment. Woodlice, too, represent dim, unresponsive foot soldiers of the worst sort, just as likely to nibble their own side's rations as yours. Understandably, no army can guarantee to stop woodlouse or slug raids and you therefore find yourself forced into the corner of saying no to lettuces.

This is a bitter pill to swallow, but in return I must offer the promise that it is most improbable that you will be expected to give up tomatoes. No enemy has ever really devised a satisfactory method of eradicating the tomato, and whilst there are many types of weapon that can dent its armour, it almost always survives in its rather dopey, sleepy way. It is just not worth anything as a bargaining tool.

So there you have it. I have done my best to guide you through the minefield of the battlefield. I have drawn on my long experience of garden warfare in the hope that others may learn by my mistakes. I have fought in many different types of terrain and all weathers. In that time I have met pretty well every type of enemy and probably seen every weapon used since the beginning of armed conflict. Fortunately, there are a few crumbs of comfort that I can offer. The first is that despite all that has been thrown at it, my own garden is still there, still a pleasant place to be and not a post-cataclysmic wasteland. It is not drenched in chemical defences, and although I have on occasion been dragged to the

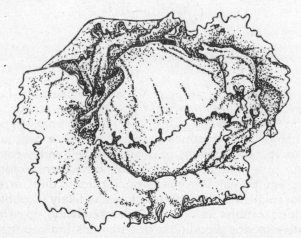

You may find yourself forced into the corner of saying no to lettuce.

negotiating chamber, I have rarely had to concede very much. But most importantly of all, despite the fierce battles that have raged in gardens up and down the land, battles in which no quarter has been asked or given, we have still been spared a victory by the ultimate deterrent, the weapons that could destroy civilised gardening as we know it. Such weapons do exist—the local pub, the golf course, the world snooker championships, the top ten, the family summer holiday, Terry Wogan, Australian soaps . . . Be vigilant always: no garden can ever really be safe while these things are allowed to exist.

Index

THIS PROUD
AND SAVAGE LAND

A vivid saga of passion, turmoil and heartache in nineteenth-century Wales

Hywel Mortymer is just sixteen in 1800, when a family feud leaves him orphaned, dispossessed and hunted even to the grim coalmines of Blaenafon, where he flees to seek survival below ground.

There he finds the elfin beauty Rhian, who labours with him at coal face and iron furnace to safeguard their love against pit disaster and vengeful cousins alike. But a harsh land lives by harsh laws and, by the shining waters where they snatched their brief joy, Hywel must confront his tormentors and their bitter, brutal vendetta . . .

Set amid the dark tangle of danger and corruption of the early days of the Welsh coal industry, *This Proud and Savage Land* is an enthralling saga of love, of treachery, and of the very land itself.

Also by Alexander Cordell in Sphere paperbacks – don't miss
TUNNEL TIGERS

0 7221 2573 9   GENERAL FICTION

— IN —
DISTANT WATERS
RICHARD WOODMAN

From the very start of her mission to the Pacific, when Captain Nathaniel Drinkwater has to hang a deserter, His Majesty's Cruiser *Patrician* is dogged by ill-luck. Mutiny is in the air, the seas of Cape Horn are cruel and Drinkwater's top-secret orders are infuriatingly vague. Even the capture of a Spanish frigate fails to stem the tide of misfortune, for the temptations of San Francisco prompt the mutinous crew to sabotage — leaving *Patrician* a helpless prize for the Spanish and their ruthless Russian allies.

But fate, in the shape of the stunningly beautiful, Dona Ana Maria, daughter of the Commandante of San Francisco and an extraordinary shift in national allegiances, offers Drinkwater one slim chance to save his ship, his mission, and his life . . .

Also by Richard Woodman in Sphere paperback — don't miss:

AN EYE OF THE FLEET
A BRIG OF WAR
THE CORVETTE
BALTIC MISSION
A KING'S CUTTER
THE BOMB VESSEL
1805

0 7474 0245 0   GENERAL FICTION

WILDTRACK

BERNARD CORNWELL

After the hell of the Falklands War, Nick Sandman, VC, knows what it is to be a hero. Barely able to walk, he's got no money, no job and no prospects. But, defiantly, he clings to the memory of a boat called *Sycorax*, his only possession, his only hope of a life at sea with no rules and no fighting. Until even that dream is shattered . . .

For there is no *Sycorax* to return to — only a beached and battered wreck, torn from its Devon mooring. In its place stands the gleaming ocean racer *Wildtrack*. And into Nick's life comes its menacing owner Tony Bannister, a rich and powerful TV personality. Compelled to make a desperate bargain with the ruthless Bannister, Nick is forced into a deal which may give him a chance to reclaim his dream — but at a price. And in the murky world of deceit and fraud into which Nick is thrown, that price could be his own life . . .

Also by Bernard Cornwell in Sphere Books:
REDCOAT

0 7474 0187 X   GENERAL FICTION

SHEILA HOCKEN
AFTER EMMA

Emma the miracle guide-dog brought joy and light into the life of Sheila Hocken – and into the lives of her millions of readers. Now Emma has gone – and Sheila's sight has been restored after a successful operation. But Emma left her owner with a lifelong love of dogs and of labradors in particular.

After Emma relates more of the hilarious (and sometimes despairing) antics of the canine contingent of the Hocken household. Teak, Mocha, Bracken and Buttons vie for attention with Sheila's husband, her daughter and three Siamese cats. And it isn't long before Kate, a black labrador puppy, arrives, shortly to be followed by Elsa, a neurotic mongrel found during a shopping spree in aid of forgetting the bank manager.

Also by Sheila Hocken in Sphere Books:

EMMA & I
EMMA V.I.P.
EMMA & CO

0 7474 0119 5   AUTOBIOGRAPHY

Sphere now offers an exciting range of quality fiction and non-fiction by both established and new authors. All of the books in this series are available from good bookshops, or can be ordered from the following address:

Sphere Books
Cash Sales Department
P.O. Box 11
Falmouth
Cornwall TR10 9EN.

Please send cheque or postal order (no currency), and allow 60p for postage and packing for the first book plus 25p for the second book and 15p for each additional book ordered up to a maximum charge of £1.90 in U.K.

BFPO customers please allow 60p for the first book, 25p for the second book plus 15p per copy for the next 7 books, thereafter 9p per book.

Overseas customers including Eire please allow £1.25 for postage and packing for the first book, 75p for the second book and 28p for each subsequent title ordered.